Napoleon's
LOST FLEET

A ROUNDTABLE PRESS BOOK

Napoleon's LOST FLEET

Bonaparte, Nelson, and the Battle of the Nile

LAURA FOREMAN
ELLEN BLUE PHILLIPS
FOREWORD BY FRANCK GODDIO

DISCOVERY COMMUNICATIONS, INC.

John S. Hendricks
Founder, Chairman, and
Chief Executive Officer

Judith A. McHale
President and
Chief Operating Officer

Michela English
President
Discovery Enterprises Worldwide

Raymond Cooper
Senior Vice President
Discovery Enterprises Worldwide

DISCOVERY PUBLISHING

Natalie Chapman
Vice President, Publishing

Christine Alvarez
Business Development
and Operations

Kimberly Small
Senior Marketing Manager

Rita Thievon Mullin
Editorial Director

Mary Kalamaras
Senior Editor

Maria Mihalik Higgins
Editor

Michael Hentges
Art Director

Heather Quinlan
Editorial Coordinator

Discovery Communications, Inc., produces high-quality television programming, interactive media, books, films, and consumer products. Discovery Networks, a division of Discovery Communications, Inc., operates and manages the Discovery Channel, TLC, Animal Planet, and Travel Channel.

ROUNDTABLE PRESS, INC.

Directors: Susan E. Meyer, Marsha Melnick, Julie Merberg
Art Director: Richard J. Berenson, Berenson Design & Books Ltd.
Production Editor: John Glenn
Photo Research: Picture Research Consultants
Consultants: Colin White and Professor William S. Cormack
with additional thanks to William Cogar, Donald Horward, David Roberts,
Geoffrey Parker, John Lynn, George Constable, Virginia Croft, Helen Garfinkle

Library of Congress Cataloging-in-Publication Data

Foreman, Laura.
   Napoleon's lost fleet : Bonaparte, Nelson, and the Battle of the
Nile / Laura Foreman, Ellen Blue Phillips ; foreword by Franck
Goddio.
      p.   cm.
   Includes bibliographical references and index.
   ISBN 1-56331-831-8 (hardcover)
   1. Nile, Battle of the, 1798.   2. Napoleon I, Emperor of the
French, 1769-1821--Military leadership.   3. Nelson, Horatio Nelson,
Viscount, 1758-1805--Military leadership.   I. Phillips, Ellen Blue.
II. Title.
DC226.N5F67   1999
940.2'742--dc21   99-33398
                                                      CIP

Random House website address: www.atrandom.com
Discovery Communications website address: www.discovery.com
Printed in the United States of America on acid-free paper
10 9 8 7 6 5 4 3 2 1
First Edition

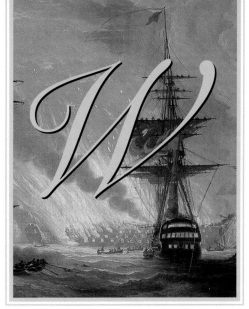

FOREWORD

WHEN AN EVENT IN HISTORY leaves behind a priceless piece of itself—a journal page, a map, a leather shoe, a ship's wooden skeleton—it is something worth noting. But when history leaves behind an entire trove of these remnants, allowing us to see the past as though looking through a window, it is truly something for all of us to celebrate. Such is the fortune surrounding a searing bit of eighteenth-century naval history. The Battle of the Nile in 1798 was the culmination of a high-stakes cat-and-mouse chase that plays out again on the pages of this book.

My own fascination with this battle began when I was a boy growing up in France, where I used to spend vacations in the family home of descendants of a wildly fascinating man: Admiral Aristide Aubert Dupetit-Thouars, commander of the ill-fated *Tonnant*, which was attacked along with the rest of Napoleon's fleet by the brilliant Lord Nelson and his British squadron during the Battle of the Nile. His last words were "Crew of the *Tonnant*, never surrender." As an impressionable child on holiday, I was surrounded by heirlooms of Dupetit-Thouars, including a romantic marble relief representing that dramatic episode.

In 1983 French marine explorer Jacques Dumas began the task of locating and excavating the wrecks of the ships sunk during the battle that had resonated in my childhood imagination so long before. Numerous attempts had been made over the years to find these wrecks, but it was Jacques's electronic

Project Director
Franck Goddio

Clutching an encrusted musket found on the floor of Egypt's Aboukir Bay, Jean-Claude Roubaud, a diver with Franck Goddio's excavation team, surveys military detritus from the Battle of the Nile. In front of him, ammunition balls fan out around a half-buried sword.

survey of the area, done with the help of the French navy, that put the ships' treasures and secrets within reach. He succeeded in locating Bonaparte's 124-cannon flagship, the *Orient*. Jacques also found the 40-cannon frigate, *Artémise*, that was set ablaze at her captain's orders on the second day of the battle.

At the time, I was conducting a study of underwater excavation activities then underway around the world. When I met Jacques Dumas, who later became my friend, he invited me to visit the excavation site in July 1984. I was thrilled to be able to dive there—my first dive on an archaeological site—as I knew that the *Tonnant* had been next in line from the *Orient*. There I saw, for the first time, important wooden remains of the once-grand ship and huge cannons. Soon Jacques and I decided to work together on further underwater recovery efforts. Sadly, Jacques died a few months later, before we were able to begin a joint project in the Philippines. I later embarked on several underwater archaeological excavations there, including one of the Spanish galleon *San Diego,* which sank in 1600.

In 1996 I returned to Egypt, where I began an exhaustive survey of Aboukir Bay to locate submerged ruins. During this survey we again located not only the site of the *Orient* and the *Artémise* but also that of another frigate, the *Sérieuse,* sunk during the same battle. In 1998, at the request of the Egyptian Supreme Council for Antiquities, my team and I resumed excavation of the *Orient* and began work on the remains of the *Sérieuse.* On the night of August 1, 1998, exactly two centuries after the battle, we were anchored at the site of the drama—and the story of Nelson and Bonaparte began to play out once again.

An eighteenth-century engraving offers an imaginative view of Bonaparte's landing at Alexandria in 1798: a friendly local official presents him with the keys to the city (left). In reality, the French troops marched on Alexandria and conquered it by force of arms.

Franck Goddio
Paris, 1999

NAPOLEON	DATE	NELSON
	September 29, 1758	Born.
Corsican partisans expel Genoese.	*1761*	
Born.	*August 15, 1769*	
Genoa cedes Corsica to France.	*1768*	
	1771	Joins *Raisonnable* as midshipman under Captain Maurice Suckling, his uncle.
	June 1773	Joins expedition to Arctic.
	April 1777	Promoted to lieutenant.
Attends Brienne on scholarship.	*1778*	
Graduates from Ecole Militaire in Paris and attends artillery school at Valence.	*1786*	
Often on paid leave in Corsica attending to family affairs.	*1786-1788*	
	1787	Marries Frances Nisbet on Nevis.
	1787-1793	Lives with Frances and his father on half pay at Burnham Thorpe, desperate for a ship.
Back in Corsica organizing Republican revolt.	*1789*	
Bonaparte family arrives in Marseilles as refugees.	*1793*	
National Convention establishes republic and is at war with Austria, Great Britain, Holland, and Spain.	*1793*	
	January 30, 1793	Assigned his first ship of the line command, the 64-gun *Agamemnon*.
	February 1, 1793	France declares war on England.
Toulon falls to Napoleon and Republican army.	*December 19, 1793*	
Republican army conquers Low Countries.	*1794*	
	January 1794	Nelson joins Admiral Hood at Corsica in a campaign of coastal raids.
	May 21, 1794	Corsican town of Bastia falls after 37-day bombardment.
	July 12, 1794	Nelson loses sight in right eye during siege of Calvi.
Maximilian Robespierre falls; Reign of Terror ends.	*July 27, 1794*	
	August 12, 1794	Calvi falls to the British.
	March 11, 1795	Nelson badly cripples *Ça Ira*, the French 84-gun, in a fleet action.
Napoleon in Paris working on plan for invasion of Italy.	*Summer 1795*	
Puts down Vendémiaire insurrection and is appointed commander in chief of the Army of the Interior.	*October 1795*	
Assigned command of the Army of Italy.	*1796*	
	March 1796	Appointed commodore and assigned 74-gun *Captain*.
Marries Josephine.	*March 9, 1796*	
Departs for Italy.	*March 11, 1796*	
Piedmontese sue for armistice.	*April 23, 1796*	
After smashing Austrian rear guard at Lodi, Napoleon enters Milan.	*May 14, 1796*	
Mantua capitulates.	*February 1797*	
	February 14, 1797	British decisively beat Spanish in a fleet battle off Cape of St. Vincent; Nelson personally captures two Spanish ships and is given a knighthood. After the battle, news reaches Nelson that he has been promoted to rear admiral.
Austria agrees to preliminary peace treaty.	*April 1797*	
	July 24, 1797	Leads disastrous invasion of Santa Cruz, in which 139 seamen and marines are killed. Injured right arm is amputated after the action.
Treaty of Campo Formio is concluded with Austria.	*October 1797*	
Directory orders Napoleon to plan conquest of Egypt.	*March 1798*	
	April 1798	St. Vincent dispatches Nelson to Toulon with force of three frigates and three 74s.
Napoleon and French fleet depart Toulon with Vice Admiral Brueys.	*May 19, 1798*	
	May 20, 1798	Nelson's ships are caught in storm 75 miles off Toulon. The *Vanguard* is seriously crippled.
General d'Hilliers joins fleet at Gulf of Genoa.	*May 21, 1798*	
Vaubois's division picked up along Corsican coast.	*May 27, 1798*	
Desaix's convoy joins fleet from Civitavecchia.	*May 28, 1798*	
	June 5, 1798	St. Vincent dispatches 10 additional 74s and one 50-gun ship to join squadron and directs Nelson to find and stop Napoleon.
French invade Malta.	*June 10, 1798*	Squadron checks Genoa, proceeding southeast along Italian coast.
Knights (of the Order of the Knights Hospitalers of Saint John of Jerusalem) ask for truce.	*June 12, 1798*	
	June 13, 1798	Nelson learns from a Tunisian warship that French were off Sicily nine days earlier, heading east. Soon he hears of the fall of Malta.
Napoleon departs Malta for Egypt.	*June 19, 1798*	
	June 22, 1798	Off southern tip of Sicily, Nelson is told by a passing brig that French left there six days earlier; however, brig's information is wrong: French fleet passed through just three days before—in fact, outlying edge of French armada is fewer than 30 miles away.
French fleet hears British signaling gunfire in Ionian Sea.	*night of June 22, 1798*	
	June 28, 1798	Nelson arrives in Alexandria to no sign of the French. Sails east and then north, past Syria.
French land at Marabout Bay.	*night of June 30, 1798*	
French march on and take Alexandria.	*July 1, 1798*	

NAPOLEON	DATE	NELSON
Brueys moves French fleet from Alexandria to Aboukir Bay.	July 7, 1798	
French defeat Mamelukes after 19-day march in the desert.	July 21, 1798	Nelson puts into Syracuse for supplies.
Napoleon enters Cairo.	July 24, 1798	
	July 25, 1798	British sail east again, searching desperately for Napoleon.
Brueys appeals to Napoleon for fresh supplies.	July 26, 1798	
	August 1, 1798	The *Alexander* and *Swiftsure*, Nelson's advance ships, arrive in Alexandria and see French tricolor flying in town.
	2:45 p.m., August 1, 1798	The *Zealous* and *Goliath* signal Nelson that French lie in Aboukir Bay.
	5:30 p.m., August 1, 1798	Nelson signals British fleet to "form a battle line as most convenient." British fleet engages French fleet in Battle of the Nile.
	10:00 p.m., August 1, 1798	The *Orient*, Napoleon's flagship, explodes. Only 60 seamen from ship's 1,000-strong complement survive; Admiral Brueys is killed.
	August 1798	Nelson imposes a blockade of Egypt. Napoleon sends communiqué to France blaming Brueys for defeat. After battle, Nelson is internationally acclaimed.
	September 22, 1798	The *Vanguard, Culloden,* and *Alexander* arrive in Bay of Naples for repairs; Nelson becomes guest of Emma and Sir William Hamilton.
Napoleon puts down rebellion in Cairo sparked by news of Ottoman Empire joining war against France.	October 1798	
	November 6, 1798	British government awards him a baronetcy, making him Baron Nelson of the Nile.
	December 1798	Nelson evacuates Neapolitan royal family and Hamiltons from Naples to Palermo after defeat of King Ferdinand by French forces.
Captures Jaffa, beginning campaign against Ottoman Empire.	March 7, 1799	
Haifa falls to Napoleon.	March 16, 1799	
Napoleon withdraws to Cairo after two-month-long siege against Acre.	May 17, 1799	
	June 24, 1799	Nelson and his seven-ship squadron sail from Palermo to Naples to finish clearing out French influence and restore monarchy.
	June 1799	Disobeys Lord Keith's order to sail to Minorca and aid in its defense.
Defeats Turkish and British forces at Aboukir Bay.	July 25, 1799	
Accompanied by a few aides and generals, Napoleon runs the blockade for France, deserting his army.	August 24, 1799	
Arrives in France to a frenzied reception and is courted by leading political factions.	October 9, 1799	
Allied with the party of moderate Emmanuel Sieyès, Napoleon overthrows radical elements in French legislature. Within one month, he effectively overthrows Sieyès and establishes a new constitution and government.	November 9-10, 1799	
Becomes first consul.	December 17, 1799	
	February 18, 1800	Nelson captures the *Généreux*, one of the French ships that escaped from the Nile.
	July–November 1800	Returns to England with Hamiltons.
	January 1, 1801	Promoted to vice admiral of the Blue.
	April 2, 1801	British victory at the Battle of Copenhagen.
Creates peace with England through Treaty of Amiens.	March 27, 1802	
	May 14, 1803	Appointed commander in chief of Mediterranean fleet.
	May 16, 1803	Britain declares war on France.
	July 6, 1803	Nelson joins British blockade of Toulon.
Crowns himself emperor of France.	December 2, 1804	
	December 14, 1804	Spain declares war on Britain.
	March 30, 1805	French fleet escapes Toulon with British in pursuit.
	August 20, 1805	French fleet rendezvous with Spanish off Cádiz.
	October 21, 1805	Battle of Trafalgar: Nelson engages French and Spanish fleets off Cape Trafalgar on Spain's southern coast. It is a decisive British victory with 18 French and Spanish ships destroyed or captured. Nelson is hit by a musket ball and dies assured of his triumph. His last words: "Thank God I have done my duty."
Divorces Josephine and marries Marie Louise, daughter of Austrian emperor.	1810	
Invades Russia with grand army of 450,000.	June 1812	
With only 40,000 soldiers remaining, the French struggle home.	December 1812	
Coalition of European powers invades France. Napoleon is forced to abdicate and sent into exile on Elba, near Corsica.	1814	
Napoleon escapes and raises an army. Europe declares him an outlaw and brings him down at Battle of Waterloo. Napoleon is sent to St. Helena in South Atlantic. He lives out remaining years with small circle of supporters, closely guarded by British.	1815	
Napoleon dies.	1821	

GUNFIRE IN THE

French ships lie outside Alexandria in this engraving by Desaulx, one of dozens of painters, geographers, botanists, mathematicans, and historians who sailed with Bonaparte's Egyptian expedition.

Inset left: André Dutertre made the sketch of young Bonaparte for this ivory miniature aboard the flagship Orient as she sailed the Mediterranean.

Inset, right: Sir Horatio Nelson is shown here in a portrait by Lemeul Abbot, painted two years before the Battle of the Nile.

MIST

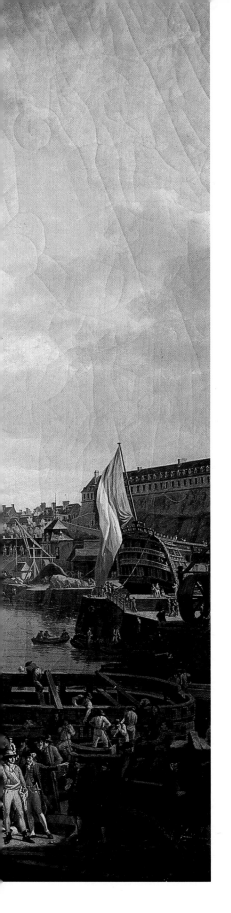

O N THE EVENING OF JUNE 22, 1798, as often in the summer, the Ionian Sea lay under heavy fog, a rising mist that enveloped the great ships passing into its waters, transforming them into a ghost fleet, mere glimmers of gray in the darkness. This spectral company was General Napoleon Bonaparte's grandiose armada—thirteen ships of the line with their attendant frigates, plus two hundred and eighty troopships in convoy. They were following an easterly course from Malta that would take the fleet along the southern shore of Crete and into the path of the *meltemi*, the summer wind that sweeps down from the north. Its gusts would drive them straight south to their goal. The French were bound for Egypt, bent on conquest. Seizing that country was only a means to a greater end, however. Power in Egypt meant leverage over Mediterranean shipping; it also meant control of the overland route to the Red Sea and India, a crucial source of wealth for Britain, France's great enemy. To wrest away India's riches would be a strategic masterstroke.

Caution was in order, however. Although Egypt lies due southeast of

This eighteenth-century painting shows the inner harbor at Brest, lined with warehouses and dockyards and crowded with ships of the line. Brest, on the western tip of Brittany, had been the French navy's chief northern port since the reign of Louis XIV; it was hard to supply, however, and the long British blockade of the 1790s strangled it.

Malta, the French fleet's commander, forty-five-year-old Vice Admiral François Paul, Comte de Brueys d'Aigailliers, had chosen the longer route via Crete at least partly as an evasive tactic. His expedition had been planned in the greatest secrecy (only forty of its officers actually knew the destination), but its scale alone ensured that the watchful British would hear of it. And in fact, only a few days earlier, Bonaparte and Brueys had learned that for the first time in two years, a sizable British battle squadron was cruising the Mediterranean, probably hunting for them.

Brueys had no desire to encounter this enemy. His battleships' crews were two thousand men short of the normal fighting complement. He was encumbered by the unwieldy transports and their thirty-eight thousand soldiers. Worse, frenetic planning had created a fleet crammed to the gunwales with arma-

While most coins carried on board the Orient *were French ones from the periods of Louis XV or Louis XVI, others were from Mediterranean countries, such as Spain.*

ments, horses, supplies, the army and its officers, Bonaparte and his staff, and hundreds of civilian scholars and their equipment. Brueys's own flagship, the magnificent three-deck, 124-gun *Orient*, sailed heavily. She was carrying nearly twice as many people as the thousand she was designed for, and their baggage cluttered her open deck. Deep in her hold, a fortune added to her weight. It included 3 million francs from the treasury of French-occupied Switzerland—gold coins stamped with the Bear of Bern would turn up in the Egyptian desert for decades—and 7 million francs' worth of gold, silver, jewels, and statuary looted from just-conquered Malta.

So Brueys was wary, and the events of that June night justified him; he was hunted indeed. Sound carries far over open water. From his own mist-shrouded quarterdeck on the *Orient*, he could hear the dull, distant booms of signal guns that the British navy used to maintain contact during fog.

The night wore on. The sandglass turned, the bells sounded the half hours, the night watches changed, and the lookouts in the crosstrees called down that all was well. Before dawn, the thuds of gunfire had faded away. And when the bright morning sun burned off the night mist, the French fleet found itself all alone, spread out over several square miles of glittering summer sea.

The admiral's evasive course had worked. The paths

of the two fleets had diverged during the night. Wherever the British now were, they no longer presented an immediate threat.

With the danger past, life aboard the *Orient* continued in its interesting, if overcrowded, fashion. Everything centered on General Bonaparte, a thin, pale, sharp-featured man who had risen to power with astonishing swiftness during the wars of the French Revolution. Bonaparte was only twenty-eight, very rough around the edges, with a harsh Corsican accent and a decided lack of grace. Even though he tended toward seasickness—a special bed with a gimballing arrangement was built for him to reduce this—he vibrated with energy, with authority, with curiosity. His aides-de-camp, his generals, and his captains flocked to his great sunlit cabin, high over the shining sea. They lay about in the adjoining divan-lined chamber where he had stored his camp library. This was a large one: Bonaparte had been trained in military schools, but his education came from his own immense reading. The library contained everything from treatises on fortification and fireworks to the three volumes of *Cook's Voyages*. Its history section included Plutarch, Tacitus, Thucydides, Arrian, and biographies of Marlborough, Peter the Great, and Frederick II. Among his choices in poetry were works by Tasso, Ariosto, Homer, Virgil, and the romantic forgeries attributed to an ancient bard named Ossian—epic tales

A 1794 pen-and-ink sketch by Philip James de Loutherbourg displays the might and beauty of French ships of the line (vaisseaux), *among the best-designed vessels afloat. This one was the* Montagne. *Like Bonaparte's flagship, the* Orient, *she was a powerful three-decker.*

of Irish heroes that were great favorites of the general. Under "politics and morals" he included the Bible and the Koran. He also collected fiction, including forty volumes of English novels. However, when he found his generals reading Goethe's *Sorrows of Young Werther*, beloved in his own earlier days, he was outraged: "Reading fit for chambermaids," he snarled. "Men should read only history."

Bonaparte himself liked to be read to. His overworked secretary, Louis de Bourrienne, did it by the hour. And the general enjoyed conversation. Despite relentless administrative work—he was planning the capture, colonization, and administration of Egypt—he gave daily dinners in the cabin, inviting different people for what amounted to either monologues or interrogations by himself, all helped along by the considerable stock of wine from Burgundy that Bourrienne had supplied. Bonaparte delighted in discourse on the subject of his own fame; he also talked obsessively about his new wife, Josephine de Beauharnais: "Josephine almost always formed the subject of our intimate conversations," Bourrienne would recall. "Passionately as he loved glory—both France's and his own—still Josephine engrossed much of the thought of a soul dedicated to vast designs. His attachment to her bordered on idolatry." The general liked after-dinner debates on subjects of his own choosing—religion, government, the art of war, whether the planets were inhabited, the interpretation of dreams. He questioned his scholars on chemistry and mathematics. He queried his captains, especially Brueys, about the finer points of seamanship and fighting sail.

There could hardly have been a better source than Brueys. The son of an aristocratic family from Languedoc in southwest France, he had been a naval officer most of his life. As a youth he had fought the Barbary Corsairs in the Mediterranean; he had served against the British in the West Indies as well; and he went on to become the captain of a dispatch vessel there. He was among the few naval officers not to emigrate during the Revolution (most French naval officers were aristocrats) and by 1792 had become the captain of a 74-gun ship of the line. Although he had been dismissed and arrested during the period of bloody excess known as the Terror, he returned to duty in 1795, helping to reform the mutinous revolutionary navy. That year he also commanded a squadron based at Corfu, which supported Bonaparte's campaigns in Italy. His performance earned him promotions to rear admiral and vice admiral and made him a natural choice for naval command of the Egyptian expedition.

As Bonaparte's secretary discovered, this "brave and unfortunate" man was near despair about the Egyptian venture. "He complained bitterly of the imperfect manner in which the fleet had been prepared for sea; of the encumbered state of the ships of the line and frigates, and especially of the *Orient*; of the great number of transports; of the bad outfit of all the ships and the weakness of their crews," Bourrienne would one day write. "He often declared, that in the event of our falling in with the enemy, he could not answer for the consequences."

*   *   *

Brueys was no coward; in his case, discretion was certainly the better part of valor. The English navy had ruled the seas for generations, and it was a general French strategy to avoid battle with it if possible.

Even with their matchless navy, however, the British had been under great pressure since 1796, when the revolutionary French had conquered northern Italy and might have invaded Ireland, had they not been halted by bad weather. The commander in chief for the Mediterranean, Sir John Jervis (soon to be Lord St. Vincent), had to withdraw his overstretched fleet from those waters that year in order to keep an eye on the Spanish, newly entered on the side of the French; he stationed his ships off Cádiz, from where he could give some support to Portugal, Britain's only remaining ally. But by 1798 the British Admiralty was receiving ominous intelligence about vast military preparations in France's Mediterranean ports. No one knew what the enemy had in mind—and the French planted false rumors in the newspapers to keep confusion high—but something clearly had to be done.

In April 1798, therefore, St. Vincent sent a reconnaissance force in to cruise off Toulon and find out what was going on. Its commander, on the 74-gun *Vanguard*, accompanied by two 74s and three frigates for scouting, was Rear Admiral Sir Horatio Nelson, thirty-nine years old, blind in one eye, and missing his right arm. He was not the most senior admiral in the navy, but he was famous for his zeal and, after a spectacular action off the coast of Spain, for his dash and courage. By 1798 he was a national hero. Fervently patriotic, royalist to the core, eager for glory, he hated the revolutionary French. Few could have viewed an adversary with such passionate determination as Nelson.

Determination did him little good at the beginning, however. His squadron, heading for Toulon, was blown off course and severely battered by a gale that blew up on May 20; the *Vanguard* was dismasted, and Nelson's frigates, assuming their commander would retreat to Gibraltar for repairs, sailed back to base. The *Vanguard* was towed to the coast of Sardinia, though, and jury-rigged for action. As for the frigates, those swift, useful eyes of a fleet, they never reappeared, and Nelson fretted constantly over them.

Things soon looked up. Under orders from the Admiralty, St. Vincent had sent some of his finest vessels to join Nelson. The little squadron became a fleet, now embracing a total of thirteen 74s and the 50-gun *Leander*.

Not only were their commanders top rate; they included some of Nelson's oldest, most trusted friends. Their orders were to proceed "in quest of the Armament preparing by the enemy at Toulon and Genoa. . . . On falling in with the said Armament, or any part thereof, you are to use your utmost endeavours to take, sink, burn, or destroy it."

The problem was to find this "Armament." While Nelson fought the storm, Bonaparte and his ships left Toulon. No one knew where he was, and even an armada could be elusive. The Mediterranean spreads over 960,000 square miles. On a perfectly clear day, a lookout in the crosstrees near the *Vanguard*'s masthead could see the horizon 12 miles distant; the topsails of a fighting ship might be visible 10 miles beyond that, meaning that on a good day Nelson's ship could survey 1,400 square miles. The French fleet was hardly a speck in such immensities.

So Nelson began cruising, interrogating every vessel he chanced upon. By June 18 he was off Naples, heading through the Strait of Messina toward Malta. He knew that if Bonaparte planned to take Sicily—a strong possibility—the French would need Malta, a magnificently fortified island commanding the Mediterranean trade routes and known since ancient times as the very "Navel of the Sea." Two days later a Genoese captain told him that Bonaparte had indeed conquered Malta and had left it six days earlier, destination unknown.

Although Sicily was the most probable candidate, the French might have another strategic target in mind. "If they pass Sicily," wrote Nelson, "I shall believe they are going on their scheme of possessing Alexandria."

Such a scheme was a problem the British had considered; French possession of Egypt not only would be a step toward complete control of the Mediterranean but would threaten British territories in India.

Nelson soon learned that the French had in fact passed Sicily and were heading east. That information was all the admiral needed. Bitterly aware that people at home would be saying he had let the French take Malta and then had lost track of their fleet, he turned directly southeast for Egypt. He could not know that the Genoese captain had been wrong: the French had left Malta three, not six, days earlier. He could not know that the armada was taking a diversionary course, and he was unaware how closely he approached them during the foggy night of June 22.

In sparkling sunshine the British fleet crowded sail, and the wind sang in the rigging. Discipline was tight; the guns were run out every day for drill. Tension was high, every soul straining toward the battle that must come, and highest of all in the admiral. "Some days must now elapse before we can be relieved of our cruel suspense, and if at the end of our journey we find that we are upon a wrong scent, our embarrassment will be great indeed," one of Nelson's captains wrote.

They covered the 700 miles in six days. Alexandria, crumbling and squalid, dozed in the summer heat. Except for an old Turkish man-of-war and some merchant ships, its harbors were empty.

The situation was extremely puzzling. According to the information they had, the British should either have overtaken the French or found them in Alexandria. Nelson sent one of his most trusted captains, Thomas Hardy, into the city to find the British consul for questioning. As fate would have it, the man was out of town. His vice consul knew nothing about any French fleet and could not get permission for the British to enter Alexandria's harbor.

His nerves at fever pitch, his spirit unable to bear inactivity, Nelson left the environs of Alexandria on June 28 and took his fleet east, hunting along the coast. Twenty-five hours later Bonaparte landed in Alexandria. As Nelson would write about his enemy, "The devil's children have the devil's own luck."

Within a month, however, the great fleets would come together in one of the epic clashes of the age of fighting sail. The two men who did most to bring it about—Bonaparte and Nelson—would never actually meet, yet they were the principals, brought into oblique but violent collision by the currents of history and chance.

The two men were different in background, talent, and character. Nelson served one of Europe's most stable monarchies; Bonaparte, clawing his way up through the chaos of Revolution, served mainly himself. Nelson craved honor and fame as a defender of his country; Bonaparte craved personal power and an empire to rule. In one way, however, they were alike: both saw themselves as men of destiny. Now those dreamed-of destinies stood in direct opposition, edging toward a battle whose thunder would echo far across the world's stage and down through the years.

Pursued by vengeful Republican soldiers, French rebels flee toward British ships in a contemporary engraving called The Capture of Toulon.

Inset: Antoine-Jean Gros's portrait of Bonaparte at Arcola romanticizes the 1796 Italian battle, during which the young general led his men into a hail of musket and cannon fire at a well-defended bridgehead.

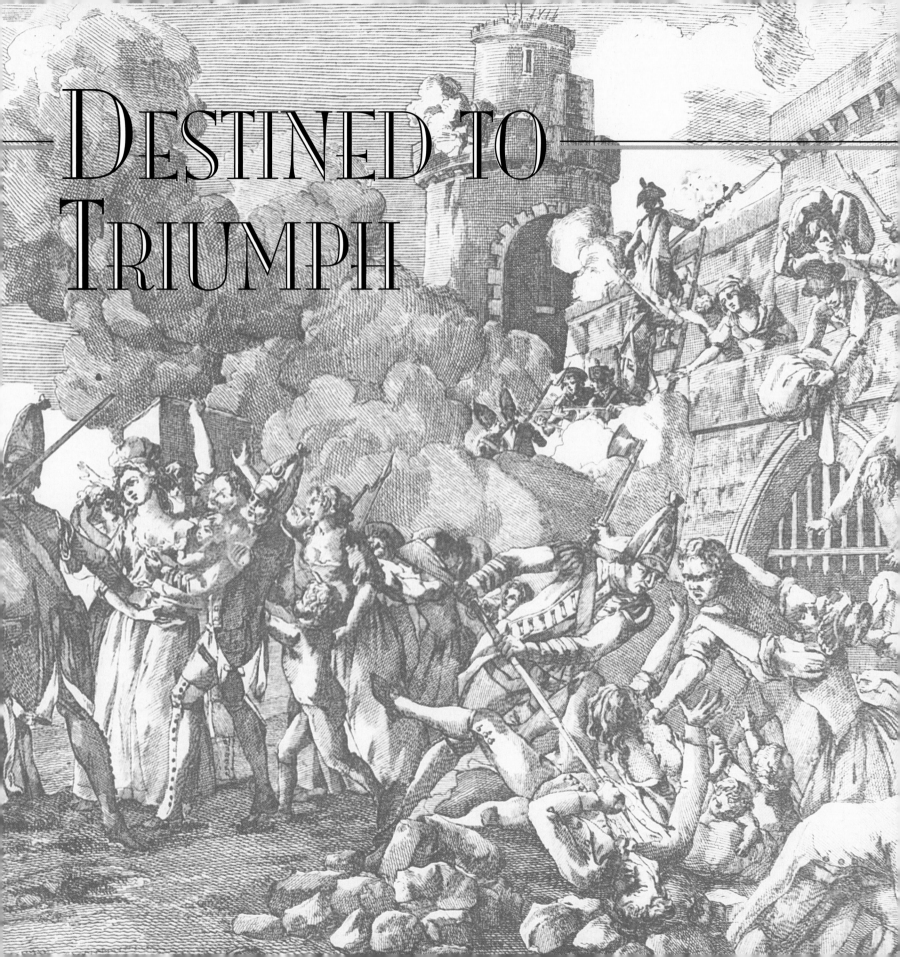

Destined to Triumph

 HE FRENCH AND BRITISH FLEETS converging in the southeast Mediterranean in the summer of 1798 were instruments of a struggle far more profound than the dynastic quarrels and territorial wars that had roiled Europe in the past. A world had been toppled in France: a king guillotined, the nobility driven out or killed, the churches closed and their priests forced to submit to the state or die, dissidents of every sort—from rich merchants to unwary men in the street—massacred. Even the calendar was remade to rid it of its Christian taint. Suddenly radical ideas and militant energies were loose, and no one could be sure what they might create or destroy.

Bonaparte's birthplace on the Strata Malerba ("Weedy Street") in Ajaccio, Corsica, is captured in a nineteenth-century watercolor. The austere facade, its shutters closed against the Mediterranean sun, was typically Corsican, as was the barely furnished interior.

Although the rest of Europe was only beginning to be aware of him, an extraordinary man would come to embody the threat of France—and relentlessly magnify it. Napoleon Bonaparte had vaulted to the threshold of power by a mixture of cunning and genius, and now he sensed boundless possibilities. The expedition to Egypt in 1798 was only a foretaste of the scope of his ambition and daring. With Egypt behind him, he would wage a kind of world war for fifteen years, leading almost invincible armies across continental Europe, inexorably absorbing princedoms into his vast shadow. Only the island of Britain, mistress of the seas, would implacably defy him.

Millions saw in Bonaparte the stuff of nightmares. Children called him "Boney the Ogre." Painters depicted him as Death. The crude British press portrayed him variously as a murderer, a rug-chewing epileptic, and a descendant of galley slaves, murderers, and whores. Yet reviewing this gallery late in life, when his triumphs were behind him, he would write, "Of all the insults heaped on me in so many pamphlets, the one to which I was most sensitive was that of being called 'the Corsican.'"

He was, as so often, rewriting his own history. Bonaparte was not in the least ashamed of Corsica. It had shaped him. Its distinctive Italian dialect was his mother tongue. The qualities of its people were threads laced deep into his character.

His island birthplace is high, dry, and stony, divided by a mountain range that sends great spurs and gorges down to the sea. To the north lies a coastal plain devoted to olive groves and vineyards; the wild southern interior, range upon lofty blue range, is impenetrable except to shepherds and the people whose isolated red-tiled villages cling to the ridges. The air is scented with arbutus, thyme, and rosemary—the dry ground cover called the *maquis*—which Napoleon would remember with nostalgia all his life.

Lying 60 miles west of the Italian coast and 100 miles southeast of the French, Corsica had always been

This sketch of Bonaparte, the earliest portrait known, shows the thin, sad face and disheveled hair that characterized him in his youth. It was drawn by a schoolmate at the Royal Military School at Brienne when the future general was sixteen.

a battlefield. Whoever controlled it, from the ancient Greeks to the eighteenth-century Genoese, dominated the western Mediterranean.

Native Corsicans, like other often-conquered peoples, dealt with the invaders as circumstances allowed. If they were strong enough, they fought the strangers off. If not, they made accommodations, profiting whenever they could from opportunity. If they had to, they withdrew into their high mountains, where they maintained their old ways, seamlessly blending their traditions and their venerable cults with the Christianity of their later rulers. They were ancestor and clan worshippers. Family blood was the deepest and only trusted bond, and vendettas—deadly clan feuds driven by vengeance—could go on for generations. Corsicans were fatalists: there was God, who might be influenced by prayer, but there was also destiny, that which was "written in the sky," as Bonaparte's own father once put it, and which nothing could alter.

All of these attitudes—the distrust of everyone but family, the violence, the pride, the thirst for power, and above all the belief in destiny—were part of Bonaparte's birthright. Fed by his genius and empowered by circumstance, they made him seem invincible, a force of nature.

He absorbed his knowledge at his parents' knees. On

this impoverished and primitive island, the Bonapartes were gentry. They owned a small country farm and a bleak town house in Ajaccio on the northwest coast; Napoleon's mother, Marie-Letizia Ramolino, and his father, Carlo Bonaparte, had useful certificates of minor Italian nobility. As Napoleon Bonaparte would comment, "We thought ourselves as good as the Bourbons; in the island, we really were."

Nevertheless, they were Corsicans and therefore subject people guided by circumstance. Carlo Bonaparte had helped expel the island's Genoese rulers in 1761, fighting in a rebel army led by a patriot named Pasquale Paoli. Seven years later Genoa ceded the difficult island to France, and after a brief, terrible guerrilla action, Paoli retreated to exile in England and Corsica became French. Both Carlo and Letizia—who, pregnant with her second son, Napoleon, had hidden with rebels in the mountains during that second wave of fighting—

swiftly made peace with their new governors, forging promising French connections.

They needed connections. Whatever his pretensions, the charming Carlo was not a good provider, and his family was poor. After Napoleon's birth on August 15, 1769, Letizia bore seven more children who survived infancy. In the crowded, sparsely furnished house, the mother ruled this huge brood then, as later, with an iron hand.

This rough and ready childhood, ragged but proud, ended for the young Bonaparte when he was almost nine. His father, using his patents of nobility and his French contacts, secured a scholarship for the boy at Brienne, one of twelve royal schools for sons of the aristocracy.

At Brienne, on the cold plains of Champagne, the boy learned at once that he was not "as good as the Bourbons." He did well in lessons, especially in mathematics, but he was a provincial who could hardly speak

French. His schoolmates turned his curious name, then spelled and pronounced "Napoleone" into *Paille-au-nez*, meaning "straw in the nose." His response was sullen. He became a combative loner who flaunted his Corsican patriotism and made Paoli his hero.

He remained proud and sullen when his father, then dying, procured him a scholarship at the Ecole Militaire, the French West Point, in Paris. Still using the Corsican form of his name, he entered in 1784 as Napoleone de Buonaparte, Esq., a student of artillery.

The school was severe but elegant, and class distinctions were evident, especially to Bonaparte, whose poverty and clumsy manners isolated him among the sons of the French aristocracy. "Civilize this dangerous islander," a drill instructor told one of his friends, to little effect. On the other hand, his artillery examiner, noting that the seventeen-year-old was well read and applied himself to the sciences, commented: "He is quiet and solitary, capricious, haughty, and frightfully egotistical. . . . He is most proud, ambitious, aspiring to everything. This young man merits our consideration and help."

Blessed with a quick mind and a prodigious memory, Bonaparte passed the course in just one year (it often took three). As he would be throughout his life, he was unsurprised by his success. It was his destiny: "Soldier I am and that because it was a special gift I was endowed with at birth," he said at the time. A second lieutenant now, he was ordered to the prestigious artillery school at Valence, in western France, where he distinguished himself in artillery theory. Unlike most roustabout junior officers, he spent his free time reading. His appetite for knowledge reached to subjects as varied as the government of the ancient Persians and the economy of England. He also filled his notebooks with apostrophes to a Corsica bound in "French chains."

Army life was hardly restrictive. The lieutenant spent three-quarters of his time from 1786 to 1788 on paid leave in Corsica, helping his widowed mother deal with financial problems. When the French Revolution broke out, he was inspired; by September 1789 he was back on the island, organizing the people along revolutionary principles. The information he sent to the National Assembly in Paris prompted its deputies to declare Corsica part of the new France, with all rights and liberties.

But the hero of his youth, Pasquale Paoli, had other ideas. Seeing an opportunity to restore Corsican independence, the exiled leader returned home to challenge the French. Corsican politics, never stable, split into a nationalist faction, led by Paoli and Corsica's priests—who objected to the anticlericalism of the Revolution—and a French revolutionary party, led by the Bonapartes. Paoli, so passionately admired by the boy Napoleon, became the adversary who blocked the man's ideals and ambitions.

As would always be the case, ambition drove Bonaparte; ideals were a lesser flame. Whatever his Corsican activities, he kept his options open and his French army commission secure. He was aware that the Revolution presented unparalleled opportunities in France. Two-thirds of the aristocratic officer corps of the infantry and a third of their artillery counterparts had emigrated. Good officers were in demand.

His hotheaded, leftist brother Lucien sensed where

THE FRENCH REVOLUTION: A CHRONOLOGY

A range of factors, from Enlightenment and Romantic philosophies to a failed harvest, fed the bloody series of French revolutions that terrified Europe and led to twenty-three years of war, but the immediate causes were taxation and self-interest. The *ancien régime* was theoretically an absolute monarchy; in reality, the nobility, clergy, and provincial governments had accumulated layers of legal privileges that severely restricted the king's authority. In 1788, crippled by the expenses of supporting the American Revolution and unable to increase revenue from an overburdened peasantry, Louis XVI's ministers attempted to tax all landowners, regardless of privileges. The effort was thwarted by the courts of the *ancien régime*. When the ministers tried to replace their representatives, an "aristocratic revolt" forced the crown to convene the Estates General—composed of the three estates of clergy, aristocracy, and commons—for the first time in 175 years. Chaos followed.

1789: THE FIRST REVOLUTION

Gathering at Versailles, the landowners who made up the commons refused to meet separately as an inferior body, as required; instead, on June 17 they declared themselves the National Assembly, abolishing the Estates General. This first assertion of the power of the people led to riots and burnings throughout France and, on July 14, to the storming of the Bastille—the royal prison in Paris notorious in literature and already scheduled for demolition—as part of a popular search for arms to defend the city from royal troops.

The National Assembly issued a Declaration of Rights on August 26, abolishing class privileges and feudal obligations but leaving Louis XVI a constitutional monarch. He was reluctant to ratify the bill. In October a mob forced him and his hated Austrian

An engraving after François Gérard memorializes the storming of the Tuileries on August 10, 1792. Enraged by losses in war and by an Austro-Prussian threat of "an unforgettable act of vengeance" if any harm should come to Louis XVI, the mob slaughtered and mutilated six hundred of his Swiss guards; the king took refuge in the Assembly.

In an anonymous engraving, executioner Charles-Henri Sanson displays the head of Louis XVI, guillotined January 21, 1793, in what is now the Place de la Concorde. To prevent demonstrations, the gates and shutters of Paris had been ordered closed, the streets lined four deep with soldiers, and the king transported in a closed carriage escorted by twelve hundred guards.

queen, Marie Antoinette, to leave Versailles for Paris, where they lived as virtual prisoners in the Tuileries Palace.

1789 TO 1791: RECONSTRUCTION

The National Assembly began to reform France, above all creating a uniform system of local government. Their confiscation of church lands, reorganization of the clergy, and demand for a clerical oath of loyalty, however, split the country into those supporting church and monarch and those supporting the new regime. The royal family attempted to escape France and failed; in the hysterical reaction that followed, amid increasing demands from the radical left for a republic, the nation edged close to civil war. The Assembly prevailed in its

moderate plans by force. The king accepted the new Constitution of 1791 and was reinstated, and the Revolution was declared to be over.

1792: THE SECOND REVOLUTION

In fact, the Assembly, like the nation, had split along political and religious lines, and its constitution quickly collapsed. Believing France's old enemy, Austria, to be fomenting counterrevolution, a new Legislative Assembly declared war. Austria's ally Prussia invaded France. Military defeats led to a second revolution in which crowds attacked the Tuileries on August 10, overthrowing the monarchy.

The Legislative Assembly ordered the election of a National Convention

to shape a new constitution; meanwhile, the Republican Commune of Paris imprisoned the royal family and crowds massacred hundreds of supposed counterrevolutionaries held in Paris prisons.

1792 TO 1793: THE NEW REPUBLIC

In the autumn of 1792, the National Convention stunned Europe by declaring France a republic, announcing a policy of revolutionary war for "the punishment of tyrants" and (the following January) executing Louis XVI.

The Convention itself was bitterly divided into Montagnards ("mountaineers," who occupied the high tiers of seats to the left of the Convention's assembly hall), led by members of radical Jacobin clubs, who sympathized with the domination of Paris; and more moderate Girondins (named for the region of France where many came from), who feared the influence of Parisian radicals. After military reverses on the borders and royalist uprisings in the Vendée, the Convention established the Committee for Public Safety to mobilize for total war and the Revolutionary Tribunal to deal with suspected counterrevolution. Following a Paris insurrection on June 2,

As Jacques-Louis David's sketch reveals, Queen Marie Antoinette went to her death on October 16, 1793, with a brave demeanor and a straight back. Anxious to spare her no indignity, the Revolutionary Tribunal had her hair cropped in prison rather than on the scaffold and ordered her sent to the executioner with her hands tied, in a common criminal's cart.

1793, the Montagnards took control of the Convention and expelled the Girondins.

1793 TO 1794: THE REIGN OF TERROR

Amid the chaos of invasion from the east, royalist uprisings in the west, and provincial revolts in the south against the "dictatorship of Paris," the Convention issued the democratic Constitution of 1793, approved by plebiscite.

Guided by the Montagnard dictum that "the republic consists in exterminating everything that opposes it" and by the fanatically virtuous Maximilien Robespierre, the Convention sent armies to subdue rebellious cities, including Lyons, Marseilles, and Toulon, and massacre their citizens. Militants closed the churches and, to help destroy Christianity, replaced the Gregorian calendar with a Republican one divided into twelve months of thirty days each, the months being named after their weather and the weeks and days after flowers, vegetables, and other blameless natural objects. The calendar was not popular, especially with the working classes, who now got only one day off in ten rather than one in seven; nevertheless, it remained in force for twelve years.

On September 5, 1793, the Terror began. Anyone not a politically correct Republican—including everyone from Girondins to royalists—could be arrested and even executed, many by the efficient and supposedly merciful machine invented by Dr. Joseph Guillotin, a deputy to the Convention. By 1794 both foreign invaders and internal rebels had been defeated, and the Terror's only object remained creating the Republic of Virtue.

The result was loathing for Robespierre, his party, and their endless bloodshed. A conspiracy of deputies overthrew him on July 27, 1794 (9 Thermidor in the new calendar), and sent him and his supporters to the guillotine the next day.

1794 TO 1795: THE THERMIDORIAN REACTION

Anarchy and inflation nearly destroyed France. Radical Republicans were unable to govern; émigré royalists failed in an attempt to invade Brittany. The National Convention finally issued the liberal Constitution of 1795, approved by plebiscite and established after Napoleon Bonaparte put down the reactionary Parisian uprising of Vendémiaire (October 5, 1795).

1795 TO 1799: THE DIRECTORY

The new constitution established a government bound to fail. It had a property owners' franchise and two legislative assemblies, but the executive consisted of five directors, who constantly plotted against one another. Purge followed coup until 1799, when the former abbé Emmanuel Sieyès, with the help of Napoleon Bonaparte—newly returned from Egypt—effected the coup d'état of 18 Brumaire (November 9 and 10, 1799).

1799 TO 1804: THE CONSULATE

Establishing the Constitution of 1799, with himself as first consul of three, Bonaparte reorganized the government and the legal and banking systems; he also restored Catholicism. In the years that followed, he steadily increased his own power and withdrew Republican rights. In 1804 he created the First Empire, ending the French Revolution.

Bonaparte's priorities lay and also where they might lead. "I have always been aware of a completely selfish ambition in Napoleone," he wrote in a letter. "He seems to me to have the potentialities of a tyrant and I believe that he would be one if he were a king, and that his name would be held in horror by posterity." Lucien Bonaparte believed in convictions. Napoleon Bonaparte preferred to sail according to the wind.

In his own way this outspoken brother would now shape events. When Paoli invited English support for Corsican independence, Lucien denounced the hero as a traitor to France. The denunciation led to a warrant for Paoli's arrest, which set off a civil war and—because nationalists far outnumbered supporters of the Revolution—sent the Bonapartes fleeing for their lives. The family's goatherds hid Napoleon (and later his mother and siblings) deep in the mountains. When Paoli turned Corsica over to the English, all the Bonapartes sailed for Marseilles. They had nothing to live on but what they could carry and Napoleon's army pay. It was the end of the young man's Corsican allegiance and the beginning of the long road he believed that destiny had prepared for him.

*   *   *

By the summer of 1793, when the Bonapartes arrived as refugees in Marseilles, the Revolution had entered its third and bloodiest phase. France had provoked war with Austria, which it suspected of aiding counterrevolutionaries, declared itself a republic, beheaded the king, and established a new National Convention to recast the constitution. The Convention, having purged itself

Exploding French ships light the sky in this engraving of the British fleet's 1793 retreat from the port of Toulon. Captain Sir Sidney Smith—whom Bonaparte would meet again at Acre—was in charge of the destruction. He sent expendable fireships, specially built for the purpose and appropriately named Vulcan *and* Conflagration, *into the French line, destroying nine capital ships, three frigates, and three corvettes.*

of moderates, was in the control of radical Jacobins, who spread their control to all of France.

The result was near disaster. The disarrayed revolutionary army was in no state to conduct a war. By the summer of 1793, Austria, joined by Prussia, had invaded France from the east. Worse, provincial France, enraged by the dictatorship of the Convention, savagely rebelled. In the west, the Vendée rose in defense of royalists. To the south, Lyons, Marseilles, and Toulon, claiming themselves Republican, rose against the Jacobins.

At this point the Jacobin faction, led by Maximilien Robespierre, seized the government, establishing the notorious Committee for Public Safety to organize an all-out war effort and put down provincial revolts. By

September Paris itself was in the grip of the Terror. The waves of executions extended to the provinces, where the Convention sent armies—supervised by its own representatives—to subdue the rebels. As France's second most important naval port, Toulon was a major target. It had opted for the monarchy and opened its harbor to a combined British and Spanish fleet. In response, the Convention's army of ten thousand swept down the coast. Napoleon Bonaparte, by now a captain, was part of it.

As luck would have it, the supervising representatives from the Committee of Public Safety included Paul

Previous page: A contemporary drawing shows Bonaparte (right) at Toulon, surveying the British fleet from the heights of Point L'Eguillette, which he had just taken. So fierce was the British defense of the harbor that the young major had a horse shot out from under him and received the only battle wound of his career—a saber cut to the thigh.

Barras, an ex-aristocrat sometimes known as the Red Viscount and now a rising Jacobin power. It also included Cristoforo Salicetti, one of Bonaparte's Corsican compatriots and a family friend. Bonaparte, seizing his opportunity, presented himself to both of them at Marseilles. He had a plan for saving Toulon—a tall order, considering the French lack of artillery and the presence of the British.

Thanks to his connections, the young captain was transferred in September to the army besieging the port. Thanks to the fact that the French artillery commander was wounded and no artillery general appeared (his orders had gone astray), Bonaparte was given a free hand; he himself became the artillery commander, with the rank of major. Thanks to his brilliant assessment of how to drive the British from the harbor, his ferocious energy in scavenging munitions for his assault, and his devotion to the job throughout—he slept, when he slept, by his thundering guns—Toulon fell. The French assault began on December 14, and the British fleet withdrew four days later. The army then rounded up all French royalists in the town square and mowed them down with cannons.

In recognition of his skill and zeal, the twenty-five-year-old Bonaparte was promoted to brigadier general. His superiors were generous in their dispatches. "Words fail me to describe Bonaparte's merits," General Jean du Teil told the minister of war. "He has plenty of knowledge, and as much intelligence and courage; and that is no more than a first sketch of the virtues of a most rare officer."

This young military paragon also proved adept at political maneuvering. Although he had been closely associated with the radical left—one of his patrons was Augustine Robespierre, brother of the terrifying Maximilien—Bonaparte survived the purge that followed Robespierre's fall on July 27, 1794, a political upheaval known as 9 Thermidor after its date on the revolutionary calendar. He even evaded efforts to post him to the wilderness of the Vendée. By the summer of 1795, Napoleon was in Paris, working for the army on a plan for the invasion of Italy.

*　　*　　*

Thermidorian Paris, as the post-coup city was called, was a perfect nurturing medium for an adventurer such as Bonaparte. Anything was possible in its fluid politics and strange social mixture of starvation and hectic gaiety. Released from the death and silence of the Terror, so poor that they bartered anything they owned for bread or firewood, Parisians launched themselves into a frenzy of activity. They thronged the theaters and dance halls, the parks and racetracks.

The mood had swung to the right in reaction to the Jacobin savagery of the Terror. Gangs of young men, mostly artisans' sons whose parents had been guillotined, roamed the streets, harassing radical deputies. They organized noisy demonstrations in the new constitutional convention. They were the *Jeunesse Dorée*—

the "golden youth" of Thermidor. In defiance of Jacobin austerities, they created the most bizarre of dandified fashions, braiding their hair into fantastic styles, swathing their necks in towering cravats, affecting the limps of old men and the lisped r's of the *ancien régime*.

The style of the *ancien régime* was in fashion among the new rulers of Paris as well. These men were survivors of the Terror, many of them liberal aristocrats, many others politicians risen from obscurity. Most were corrupt. In the midst of hunger they made fortunes on government contracts and speculation. All sought the rewards of power.

These were the men for Bonaparte. As he would say many times in later years, "There is only one thing to do in this world, and that is to keep acquiring money and more money, power and more power. All the rest is meaningless." He arrived in Paris with two companion officers, Andoche Junot and Auguste Marmont, both of whom would be with him most of his life. The three young men, with little money among them, wandered

This portrait of former viscount and corrupt Republican Paul Barras in his director's uniform of sash, lace collar, and plumes—a costume he usually refused to wear—does little justice to Bonaparte's first patron, said to be "the handsomest man of his time." Barras gave Bonaparte command of the Army of Italy and supported his Egyptian campaign in the face of great opposition.

the city, visiting theaters and restaurants, thinking up financial projects. Bonaparte alone, said Junot, made a point of "calling on anyone with influence and knocking on every door."

His most valuable friend was the powerful Deputy Barras. The Red Viscount introduced him to the places where power lay—the fashionable salons of the demimonde.

These salons intimidated Bonaparte, unused as he was to the elegancies of life. The houses where the salons took place were decorated in the severe classical mode thought to reflect the glories of ancient Rome and decreed by the painter Jacques Louis David, inventor of revolutionary design. Costumes, too, were in the antique style. Both women and men cut their hair short so that it curled around their faces, a fashion known as *à la Titus*. Even in winter, women wore tunics of the sheerest gauze and sandals on their bare feet.

Women ruled society. "Everywhere in Paris you see beautiful women," Bonaparte wrote his brother. "Here alone of all places on earth they appear to hold the reins of government. . . . A woman needs to come to

SWEET AND INCOMPARABLE JOSEPHINE

The love of Bonaparte's life was an enchanting Creole—the term then used for all white West Indians—with a shady past. Born in 1763 to a minor aristocrat and sugar planter on Martinique, Marie-Joséphe-Rose Tascher de la Pagerie had arrived in France at the age of seventeen to enter an arranged marriage with Alexandre de Beauharnais. As she soon discovered, her husband was a professed Republican and frightful snob who had awarded himself the title of viscount and classified his many mistresses by their rank. He was also brutally unkind to his wife, who, having borne two children, obtained a legal separation in 1785.

Ever tactful, never pushing, the newly freed Rose de Beauharnais used her husband's name—prominent during the early revolutionary years, when he was a deputy to and then president of the National Convention—as entrée into the world of political salons. Being fashionably Republican but with the pretty manners of the *ancien régime*, she thrived. She seems to have had several influential lovers; certainly she had many important connections by 1794, when Alexandre was imprisoned by the Revolutionary Tribunal. Never vindictive, she tried to save her husband. It was to no avail in the Terror. She herself was arrested and imprisoned in the bloodstained convent of Les Carmes with her husband. Alexandre was beheaded. Rose survived.

Thermidorian Paris, louche and pleasure seeking, was the perfect setting for her. Her best friend was the leading hostess, Thérésia Tallien. At Tallien's salon Rose met everyone of importance, including the Red Viscount, Paul Barras. In 1795, according to an acquaintance, Rose de Beauharnais was "admitted in Barras's harem."

The role of official mistress to the easygoing and generous Barras suited her, but it was to be short. Barras introduced his Corsican protégé into the salons, where he was generally ignored, except by Rose. Not long after his suppression of the riots of Vendémiaire, they became lovers. Bonaparte, dazzled by her style and elegance, insisted on marriage, which ended the liaison but not the friendship with his patron, Barras. Then he left for Italy.

"Sweet and incomparable Josephine," her husband called her in one of his passionate letters, and she was. Although at thirty-two she was considered past her prime, Josephine Bonaparte was small, slender, and always exquisitely dressed. People admired her grace: "There was a suppleness, an incredible lightness to all her movements," an admirer wrote. Then there were her eyes, "dark blue, always half closed under long lids, fringed by the longest eyelashes in the world." Most of all there was her voice, ever gentle and low, with lisped Creole r's, a voice, Bonaparte would say, "like a caress."

Josephine took the marriage lightly at first; she was amused by the torrent of letters he wrote during the Italian campaign ("I curse the glory and ambition which keeps me from the soul of my life" was one of his more temperate remarks), replying

Antoine-Jean Gros painted this portrait of Josephine Bonaparte as empress of the French.

infrequently enough to send him into frenzies of jealousy. She put off joining him.

She delayed because she herself had fallen in love with Hippolyte Charles, a dashing young Hussar with a happy nature, who—unlike her nearly humorless husband—made her laugh. The affair would continue on and off through her eventual sojourn in Milan with Bonaparte, where she was treated like a queen and where her charming manners did much to temper the impression made by his crude style. When Bonaparte left for Egypt, she continued the affair with Charles.

In Cairo, Bonaparte learned from an aide-de-camp that he was a cuckold. He was devastated. "It is sad when one and the same heart is torn by such conflicting feelings for one person," he wrote to his brother. The British seized the letter and published it. He took a mistress, known to the troops as "Cleopatra." He determined to divorce Josephine.

It was not to be. On the terrible night when Bonaparte returned from Egypt to his Paris house, he locked himself in his dressing room, refusing even to see his wife. Josephine stood outside the door, pleading for hours in her beautiful voice for forgiveness. Her son and daughter joined her. And at last, Bonaparte let her in.

For the rest of her life, Josephine was a perfect, faithful wife, always pliable and loving, adding distinction to her husband's increasingly formal consular and imperial courts. She was tolerant of his many mistresses and kind to his hostile family.

The only thing she could not do—unlike several of his mistresses—was give him a child, and this became an obsession with Bonaparte after he became emperor. In 1809, after heart-rending scenes, he divorced her and married Marie Louise of Austria the following year. She bore him the longed-for son.

Josephine carried her ill fortune with her usual grace. She retreated to the country house of Malmaison, where she remained, sweet-natured and fading, among her greenhouses, her rose gardens, and her aviaries. She died of pneumonia—or as her children preferred to call it, a broken heart—in 1814.

As for Bonaparte, he visited Malmaison to mourn just before his final exile. "She was the most alluring, the most glamorous creature I have ever known," he told her daughter, "a woman in the true sense of the word, volatile, spirited, and with the kindest heart in the world." A week before he himself died in 1821, he had a vision of Josephine. Among his last words was her name.

A crowd of solemn soldiers witnesses the divorce of Bonaparte and Josephine in this 1846 painting by Henri-Frederic Schopin. The reality was less dignified; all the Emperor's unpleasant family—his mother, sisters, and brothers—converged on his office at the palace of Fontainbleau on December 15, 1809, to observe the ceremony and gloat over the humiliation of Josephine, whom they hated.

Paris for six months to learn what is her due and to understand her own power. Here only, they deserve to control so much influence."

The favored salon, haunted by Bonaparte, was that of Thérésia, wife of the deputy Jean-Lambert Tallien. Her thatched-roof, elm-shaded house near the Seine was the stage for the beautiful, fashionable group led by a dear friend, Marie-Rose-Josephine de Beauharnais, recently released from the convent prison from which her husband had gone to "look through the Republican window," as wits liked to call beheading. Around these women, elegant and light in manner, free in behavior, all the politicians gathered. Bonaparte followed suit. Silent, sullen, small, with stringy hair and an unhealthy yellow pallor, he was hardly noticed at first. People called him "Barras's little Italian protégé" and left him alone, hovering on the edges of power.

His opportunity to move closer to the center of authority came when the National Convention finally issued its new constitution. The document decreed a five-man executive directory, of which Barras was the strong man; and a legislature composed of a Council of Elders and a Council of 500. Fearing a right-wing majority after elections, a majority that might not only undo their work but also condemn them as regicides, the Convention voted most of its own members back into legislative office. This self-protective measure roused moderate and royalist Parisians to the insurrection of Vendémiaire (October 1795) and offered Bonaparte a new opportunity to display his qualities. He might have preferred to keep his options open, but Barras called him to the Tuileries, the former royal palace

where the government now met, and gave him three minutes to choose sides. Napoleon chose Barras.

During a long night, in steady, pouring rain, the Corsican brought in his guns; by morning he had positioned his cannons on the bridges across the Seine and in the rue St. Honoré, which the crowd of twenty-five thousand would have to use to reach the Tuileries and the Convention. When the rioters charged the next afternoon, Bonaparte simply cut them down with what he described as a "whiff of grapeshot." The cannon fire left fourteen hundred bodies lying in the mud and ended the insurrection.

His reward was immediate: Barras appointed Bonaparte, now nicknamed "General Vendémiaire," as commander in chief of the Army of the Interior, with a vast new residence on the Place Vendôme and a huge salary. As ever, Bonaparte showed neither surprise nor delight. He attributed the dazzling success to the star of destiny that protected him.

Suddenly he was in demand at the salons. Madame Beauharnais—one of Barras's mistresses, as it happened—turned her famously sweet charm toward him. With all the force of his powerful nature, he fell in love, and to secure Josephine, he insisted on marriage.

Partly because of this marriage, partly because even after his success during the riots of Vendémiaire, he remained hardly known, his command of the Army of Italy drew fire when it was assigned him in 1796. Unkind critics, including his brother Lucien, for instance, claimed that Barras—who had several mistresses and treated them all amiably—was trying to get Josephine off his hands. Indeed, Barras had forced Bonaparte's appointment against considerable opposition. Lucien called the command "Barras's dowry."

The general departed for the front on March 11, 1796, two days after he and Josephine were married. No one then imagined what he would make of his command.

* * *

By the time Bonaparte left for Italy, the French had recovered from their initial military blunders—a turnabout that began back in 1793, when the country committed to total war and instituted universal conscription. The raw recruits that this policy produced were amalgamated with older units and shaped into an army of eight hundred thousand. The entire nation mobilized for their support. Great metallurgical factories worked to government orders. Even the parks of Paris—the Tuileries, the Luxembourg—became open-air foundries, fed by iron from the church bells of France.

The result was the conquest of the Low Countries in 1794. That led Prussia to seek peace, and Holland and Spain to become French satellites. But Russia, England, and the Hapsburgs' Holy Roman Empire remained at war. The Hapsburg dominion was formidable. It included not only Austria but most of the Balkans, a large part of Germany, and Lombardy and Venetia. Among its Italian allies were Savoy, Piedmont, Rome, the Papal States, and Naples.

When the Directory sent Bonaparte to Italy, it wanted to secure a French frontier at the Rhine. Two great Republican armies were to advance upon Austria from the north. Bonaparte was to invade from the south through

A sketch of Napoleon in Italy by Andrea Appiani captures the general's lean features and burning gaze. He wears the simple civilian overcoat that distinguished him as a man of the people—"son and hero of the Revolution," as foreign minister Charles-Maurice de Talleyrand-Périgord described him.

Bonaparte enters Milan in triumph in one of the nineteenth-century paintings that helped shape his legend. Having defeated Italy in battle, he commandeered a famous palace in the city as his headquarters, which he ran in the style of a royal court.

Piedmont, immobilize the southern Austrian forces, pass through the Tyrol—whose high strongholds were held by Savoy—and join the senior generals in Vienna.

The Army of Italy was then a relatively minor wing of the French forces. Even so, its generals—André Masséna, Louis Desaix, and Pierre Augereau—received their new commander with reservations at headquarters in Nice. There was speculation about "the political general." He was "stunted and sickly looking," Masséna recalled, and his manners were odd. Bonaparte introduced himself by showing around a portrait of his wife.

The initial impression was quickly dispelled by Bonaparte's forceful demeanor and by his speed in dealing with immediate problems. His usual thorough inspection showed him the state of things: "The army is in frightening penury," he wrote. "Misery has led to indiscipline, and without discipline there can be no victories." On the other hand, the soldiers were mostly volunteers and early recruits, hardened by four years of battle and strongly Republican. With the help of a forced loan from Genoa and the assistance of his old Corsican friend Cristoforo Salicetti, who was the civil commissary, the general procured supplies, including food, brandy, and twelve thousand pairs of shoes. He disbanded a mutinous battalion, leaving himself with a strike force of about thirty-eight thousand, whom he inspired with impassioned addresses, appealing to their love of glory and promising them abundant loot. Then, using theories that had never been so brilliantly deployed—the flexible line and column, the swiftly moving army that feeds off the countryside, the focused offense that sends an adversary into disarray, and above all, concentrated artillery—Bonaparte led his men to victory.

He was an electrifying leader of men, with a power some called magical. His understanding of his troops, his ferocious energy, his utter confidence in his star inspired them; his plain gray overcoat and black hat showed that he was a man of the people, like themselves. He himself was well aware of the power of his presence. He would later say it was acting, achieved by tone of voice, expression, and alternations of rage and sweetness.

Whatever it was, it created in the Republican army a magnificent spirit. August Marmont would recall it in his old age: "We marched surrounded by a kind of radiance, whose warmth I can still feel as I did fifty years ago." And he added, "There was grandeur, hope, and joy. We were all very young, from the supreme commander down to the most junior officers; all bright with strength and health and consumed by love of glory . . . we felt unlimited confidence in our destinies."

Destiny was clearly with the general; the Austrian and Piedmontese forces were widely separated. He dealt with the Austrians near the Italian coast first, driving them into the interior. Then he turned north toward the Piedmontese, who sued for armistice on April 23, fol-

lowing defeats at San Michele, Ceva, and Mondovì. By May 14 he had smashed the Austrian rear guard at Lodi and entered Milan.

Throughout the lightning campaign, he made sure that his deeds received suitable publicity back in Paris. Streams of Bonaparte's messengers arrived in the city bearing bloodstained battle flags, highly colored bulletins—"to lie like a bulletin" became a Parisian proverb—and incandescent letters to Josephine. There were also seemingly endless trains of booty to bolster the tottering French economy and the private finances of French generals. By July, Italy had already provided 60 million francs in indemnities, not to mention the art treasures of the palaces and churches of Florence, Rome, and Naples.

In the autumn Bonaparte crushed Austrian counteroffensives at Castiglione, Bassano, and Arcola; in January 1797 he was victor at Rivoli. By February, Mantua had capitulated. In April, as he moved toward Vienna to meet the armies of the Rhine, Austria agreed to a preliminary peace treaty.

"The little corporal," as his victorious troops affectionately dubbed him, was now the center of European politics. An observer reported, "He was no longer the general of a triumphant Republic, but a conqueror on his own accord, imposing his laws on the vanquished."

Indeed, he conducted himself like a head of state. When he turned his attention south toward the Papal States, the Pope ceded Bologna, Ferrara, and Mantegna—and a 30-million-franc indemnity—to prevent the kind of looting and raping the French army was famed for. Out of various remnants of Italy, Bonaparte created

STEALING THE TREASURES OF EUROPE

Every victorious army indulged in looting, but few were so methodical as the armies of Republican France. For the edification of conquered Europe, no doubt, the government issued a formal proclamation to explain its policy: "The sovereignty of all the arts should pass to France in order to affirm and embellish the reign of liberty."

To ensure that this happened, the Directory established an arts commission headed by Vivant Denon, a former courtier, pornographer, and exceptionally talented draftsman, who would accompany Bonaparte to Egypt and later organize the Louvre Museum. Denon's commissioners, among them the polymath Gaspard Monge, carefully examined foreign guidebooks to locate the best art available for France. Following their victorious armies, they then journeyed to Italy, Germany, and the Low Countries to make their selections.

The palaces and churches of Italy, seat of Roman glory and birthplace of the Renaissance, provided the cream of the captures. The bronze horses of St. Mark's Basilica in Venice (looted by the Venetians from Constantinople more than five centuries earlier) went to Paris, as did the great Lion of Venice itself. So did famous sculptures, including the Apollo Belvedere, the Laocoon, and the Medici Venus, along with one hundred artworks and five hundred ancient manuscripts from the Vatican, whose transport costs the

Pope had to pay. The best of later art was taken as well, including the Titians and Tintorettos of Venice and the Correggios of Parma and Modena.

Conquered nations did not let their heritage go without protest. In Milan, Rome, and Florence, the citizens rioted in protest. Italian noblemen tried to bribe the French. The duke of Parma, for instance, offered 30 million francs to save just one of his Correggios, and when Bonaparte and Josephine held court in Milan, gifts—from marbles and bronzes to perfect pearls and antique cameos—poured in, sent in the hopes of relief from the looting.

It was all in vain. Bonaparte, who claimed that all men of genius were French, no matter where they were born, took pride in his booty trains. He ordered a victory banner for the Army of Italy that listed his captures. It read, "Sent to Paris all the masterpieces of Michelangelo, Guercino, Titian, Paolo Veronese, Correggio, Albana, the Caracci, Raphael, and Leonardo da Vinci."

The vast collection of artworks filled the Louvre, established in a former royal palace in 1793. Denon organized it in 1804, turning it into one of the finest museums in the world.

Fortunately for the conquered nations, most of their art was returned following Napoleon's defeat at Waterloo in 1815. The French were highly indignant. They felt they were being robbed.

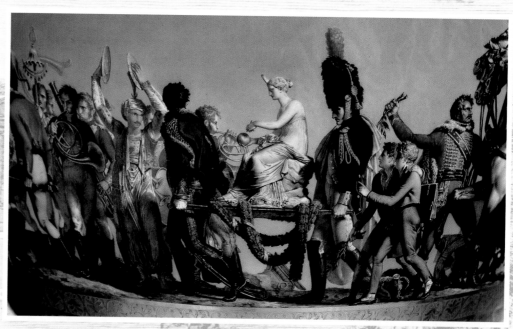

A Sèvres vase of 1813 displays Napoleonic glories. Musicians and soldiers accompany an antique Italian Venus to its new home in the Louvre Museum.

A fanciful print shows the four monumental horses of St. Mark's Basilica in Venice, looted by Bonaparte's troops, in triumphant procession (center). They are escorted by a menagerie of exotic live animals.

two new republics—the Cisalpine and the Ligurian. Peace with Austria was finally concluded with the Treaty of Campo Formio in October 1797. Bonaparte's masters at the Directory angrily agreed to it all. They had no choice.

* * *

Bonaparte was to write later that it was after his victory at Lodi on May 10 that "I realized I was a superior being and conceived the ambition of performing great things, which hitherto had filled my thoughts only as a fantastic dream." In fact, the idea of seizing supreme authority in France was already in his mind. The wild urge to play for the highest stakes, "to change the face of the world," was beginning to dominate him. But he had to deal with England, which still controlled the seas.

Dogs and looters pick among the corpses on an Italian battlefield in this painting by Nicolas Taunay. Amid the chaos, the victorious Bonaparte (mounted, center) receives the saber of a dying Austrian officer.

To this end, Bonaparte looked east. Eastern expansion was not a new idea to French geopolitical thinkers: the conquest of the Ottoman Empire had been broached as early as 1780, and in 1795 a French consul to Egypt had proposed to use that country as the pathway to British India. The idea made sense to Bonaparte, and it had other attractions. Alexander the Great had conquered Egypt. To emulate him could only advance the Corsican's rise to power. Thus in August 1797 Bonaparte advised the Directory, "The time is not far distant when we shall feel that, in order truly to destroy England, we must occupy Egypt."

In this idea Bonaparte had an ally: Charles-Maurice de Talleyrand-Périgord, the languid, intelligent cynic and great survivor, who had transformed himself from an aristocratic bishop to adviser to the Revolution to exile during the Terror. By 1797 he was minister of foreign affairs to the Directory, and he read Bonaparte's letters about an eastward expansion with interest.

Talleyrand thought an invasion of Egypt perfectly possible. While the country was formally part of the crumbling Ottoman Empire, it had been governed for three hundred years by Mameluke families. These were groups whose ancestors were military slaves from the Caucasus and Georgia; to prevent decline, they continued to buy and train slave boys as new warriors for each generation. In league with the Egyptian religious government, called the *ulama*, and with Egypt's wealthy merchants, the Mamelukes dominated a vast peasant class, which they viewed primarily as a source of taxes.

France was allied with the Ottoman Empire, and Talleyrand took the position that driving the Mamelukes out of Egypt would be doing this friend a favor. In the process, incidentally, the French would gain profitable control of the overland route to India; if the island of Malta were also conquered, the republic would dominate the Mediterranean as well.

Bonaparte concurred. "We could leave here with twenty-five thousand men, escorted by eight or ten ships of the line or Venetian frigates and take it," he wrote Talleyrand in September 1797. "Why should we not occupy Malta? The inhabitants, of whom there are more than one hundred thousand, are very well disposed to us. . . . With the island of St. Pierre, which the King of Sardinia has ceded to us, Malta, Corfu, et cetera, we shall be masters of the whole Mediterranean."

The Directory had other ideas. They appointed the conqueror of Italy commander of the "Army of England," for the purposes of invasion. But Bonaparte's coastal inspections showed that most of the warships on the Channel were neither fitted out nor crewed. It would be several years before France could even hope for mastery of the seas, and without it England was unconquerable. An expedition east would be safer and cheaper, wrote Bonaparte, and Talleyrand backed him up. By March 1798 the Directory had come around. The orders issued to Bonaparte stated that he would take possession of Egypt with his land and sea forces, "drive the English from all their Oriental possessions he can reach," cut a canal through the Isthmus of Suez, and "take all necessary measures to ensure the French Republic the free and exclusive use" of the Red Sea.

✳   ✳   ✳

The logistics of implementing this grandiose plan, directed by Bonaparte from Paris, were of nightmarish proportions. An army—of thirty-eight thousand, not the original twenty-five thousand he had mentioned in a letter to Talleyrand—had to be found and moved to various Mediterranean ports. The center of operations was Toulon, with its fortified inner harbor, capable of holding thirty ships of the line, and its well-equipped arsenal and dry dock. The army commander there was Jean-Baptiste Kléber, a tough, forty-five-year-old veteran. While Bonaparte was conquering

Italy, Kléber had been victorious in Germany. He had then retired, but Bonaparte needed him for Egypt, and by early 1798 he was in Toulon. Up the coast at Marseilles, General Jean Louis Reynier was in charge of a division. Genoa, the port next in importance to Toulon, was under thirty-three-year-old Louis Baraguey d'Hilliers. He had commanded a division in Italy under Bonaparte, and now he marched it down from Mantua to the Italian coast. Just north of Rome, at Civitavecchia, was a division under thirty-year-old Louis Desaix, like Bonaparte a minor aristocrat and highly competent professional soldier who had survived the Terror. From Corsica another Italian veteran and artilleryman, General Vaubois, would provide forty-five hundred troops.

In addition to the army and navy, there were civilians: 167 astronomers, artists, architects, engineers, and mathematicians. Bonaparte, the autodidact, was fascinated by intellectual achievement. Like Alexander before him, he saw his invasion not only as a military stroke but also as a scientific expedition, graced by the best and brightest minds. Chief among these savants were the renowned Gaspard Monge, a fifty-two-year-old mathematician and polymath, ardent revolutionary, and admirer of Bonaparte; the chemist Claude-Louis

Berthollet; and to study political economy, Jean-Lambert Tallien. They would provide the legacy of the expedition, but their extensive libraries and equipment complicated its voyage.

For the army matters were complicated enough. There were steady desertions. Money problems led to every kind of shortage, from food and water to hammocks for the officers to transportation. Most transports were merchant ships, and most of them were inadequate, as Reynier pointed out: "The vessels . . . for the

Gaspard Monge, painted here by Jean-Baptiste Mauzaisse, was the leading light among the savants whom Bonaparte took to Egypt. A famed mathematician, chemist, and physicist, Monge was also a convinced Republican whose affection for Bonaparte never wavered. He saw the commander in chief as an adopted son.

transport of the division I command are very small and can carry 100 to 200 men each. They are overloaded with artillery and equipment, some of which encumbers the decks already set aside for the billeting of the number of men which have to be put there. The officers must board the same ships as the troops they command."

The navy, which was to escort the transports, had problems of its own. Vice Admiral Brueys's warships, built in the admirable shipyards of the *ancien régime,* were being readied in the dockyards of Toulon. Although his request for reinforcements from the northern Brest squadron had been denied because the ships were needed to divert British forces from secret Mediterranean activity, Brueys's fleet was still a handsome one, with nine 74-gun warships (the *Peuple Souverain, Heureux, Spartiate, Aquilon, Guerrier, Mercure, Timoléon, Généreux,* and *Conquérant*—the last only lightly armed because its structure was weak); and three 80s (the *Tonnant, Franklin,* and *Guillaume Tell*). His superb three-deck, 124-gun flagship was a floating record of political change. She had begun as the *Dauphin Royal.* During the Revolution's radical phase, in 1792, she had been rechristened *Sans Culotte,* after the nickname for working-class revolutionaries, who wore trousers rather than aristocratic knee breeches. Now she was called—appropriately enough, given where she was now headed—the *Orient.*

Brueys also had a healthy complement of frigates for scouting duties and for herding transports; his problem was not a lack of ships, but manning those he had. The navy was only just recovering from the emigration or execution of its officers during the Revolution—the expertise required of naval officers made them much harder to replace than army commanders—and the financial problems of the government induced long-unpaid seaman conscripts to desert. For the Egyptian venture the navy drafted fishing-boat skippers,

An engraving of the period captures the chaos of the Egyptian expedition's departure from Toulon. Besides the difficulty of loading men, horses, supplies, and artillery, the French commanders had to cope with conflicting intelligence about the British fleet, reported variously to be off Minorca, between Tunisia and Sardinia, and along the route to Malta.

masters of small coasters, and privateers, mostly from the Mediterranean area. This was not only ineffective but caused enormous resentment. In the end, Brueys had enough men to sail his ships but not to fight. During the voyage he sprinkled soldiers among the gun crews for training.

Despite the obstacles—financial, human, and

natural (in the form of days of contrary winds)—
Brueys prepared for departure on May 19, a brilliantly
clear morning. Bonaparte proclaimed that the army,
which was to "imitate the Roman soldiers of yore who
fought Carthage on the plains and the Carthaginians on
the sea," would surpass all past services to their father-
land. To roars of acclaim from his audience, he also

promised each soldier 6 acres of land at home. Then
Brueys weighed anchor. At the other ports the rest of the
armada put out to sea.

Nothing like it had been seen since the Crusades,
if then: 5 squadrons comprising 55 ships of war of
different classes and 280 transports carrying 51,000 seamen, soldiers, and civilians; some 1,300 horses; 171

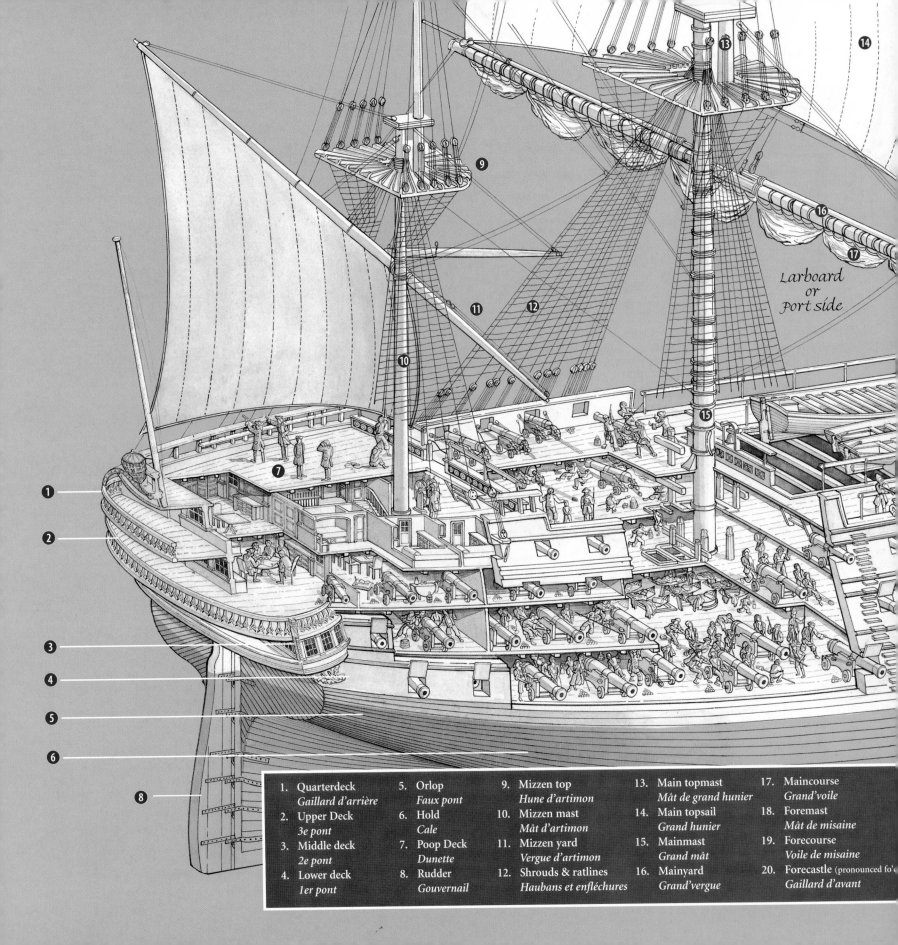

Larboard
or
Port side

1. Quarterdeck *Gaillard d'arrière*	5. Orlop *Faux pont*	9. Mizzen top *Hune d'artimon*	13. Main topmast *Mât de grand hunier*	17. Maincourse *Grand'voile*
2. Upper Deck *3e pont*	6. Hold *Cale*	10. Mizzen mast *Mât d'artimon*	14. Main topsail *Grand hunier*	18. Foremast *Mât de misaine*
3. Middle deck *2e pont*	7. Poop Deck *Dunette*	11. Mizzen yard *Vergue d'artimon*	15. Mainmast *Grand mât*	19. Forecourse *Voile de misaine*
4. Lower deck *1er pont*	8. Rudder *Gouvernail*	12. Shrouds & ratlines *Haubans et enfléchures*	16. Mainyard *Grand'vergue*	20. Forecastle (pronounced fo'c... *Gaillard d'avant*

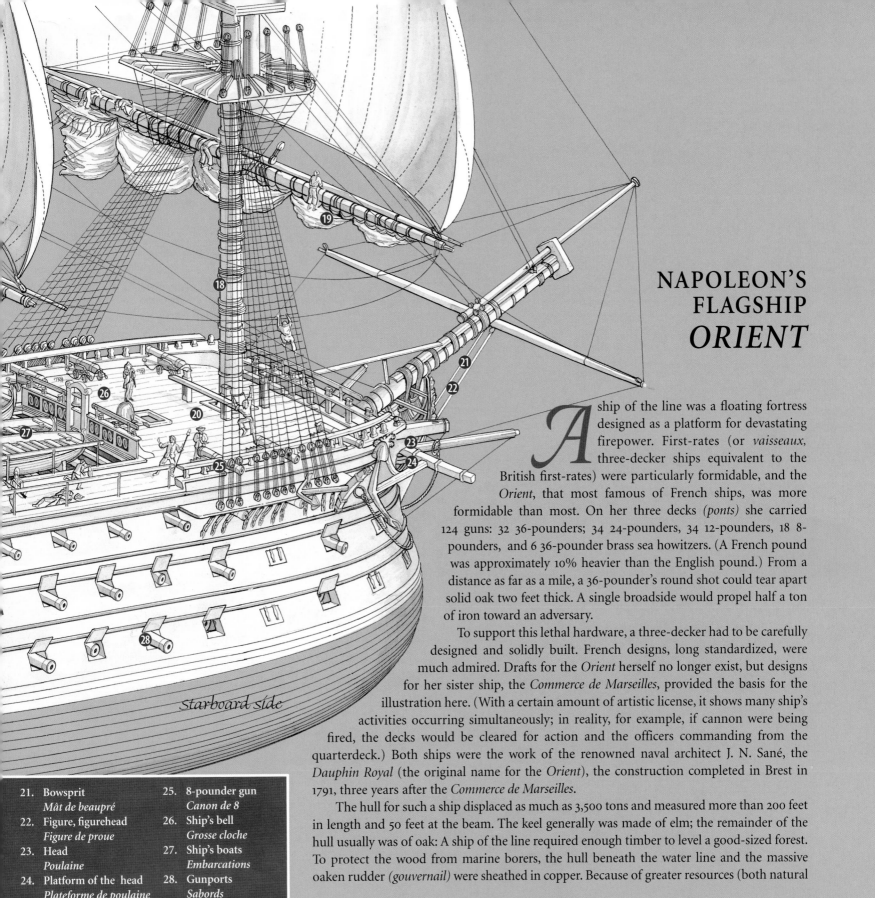

Starboard side

NAPOLEON'S FLAGSHIP
ORIENT

A ship of the line was a floating fortress designed as a platform for devastating firepower. First-rates (or *vaisseaux*, three-decker ships equivalent to the British first-rates) were particularly formidable, and the *Orient*, that most famous of French ships, was more formidable than most. On her three decks *(ponts)* she carried 124 guns: 32 36-pounders; 34 24-pounders, 34 12-pounders, 18 8-pounders, and 6 36-pounder brass sea howitzers. (A French pound was approximately 10% heavier than the English pound.) From a distance as far as a mile, a 36-pounder's round shot could tear apart solid oak two feet thick. A single broadside would propel half a ton of iron toward an adversary.

To support this lethal hardware, a three-decker had to be carefully designed and solidly built. French designs, long standardized, were much admired. Drafts for the *Orient* herself no longer exist, but designs for her sister ship, the *Commerce de Marseilles*, provided the basis for the illustration here. (With a certain amount of artistic license, it shows many ship's activities occurring simultaneously; in reality, for example, if cannon were being fired, the decks would be cleared for action and the officers commanding from the quarterdeck.) Both ships were the work of the renowned naval architect J. N. Sané, the *Dauphin Royal* (the original name for the *Orient*), the construction completed in Brest in 1791, three years after the *Commerce de Marseilles*.

The hull for such a ship displaced as much as 3,500 tons and measured more than 200 feet in length and 50 feet at the beam. The keel generally was made of elm; the remainder of the hull usually was of oak: A ship of the line required enough timber to level a good-sized forest. To protect the wood from marine borers, the hull beneath the water line and the massive oaken rudder *(gouvernail)* were sheathed in copper. Because of greater resources (both natural

21.	Bowsprit	25.	8-pounder gun
	Mât de beaupré		*Canon de 8*
22.	Figure, figurehead	26.	Ship's bell
	Figure de proue		*Grosse cloche*
23.	Head	27.	Ship's boats
	Poulaine		*Embarcations*
24.	Platform of the head	28.	Gunports
	Plateforme de poulaine		*Sabords*

and financial), the French ships tended to be better built than their English counterparts.

As for her three masts, which might rise more than 200 feet above the water, they were generally of fir—flexible in high winds—and were built in three sections. They were anchored to the hull by as much as 5 miles of standing rigging, and could carry as much as 4 acres of canvas. Shrouds and ratlines (*haubans et enfléchures*) provided ladders for the seamen who ran out along the yards to work the upper rigging and the sails.

The upper deck of a first-rate, from fore to aft, included a high forecastle (*gaillard d'avant*), a gangway that connected it to the officers' station or quarterdeck (*gaillard d'arrière*), and the lower poop deck. Beneath this open space were three decks whose entire lengths were devoted to the gunnery.

Living quarters were tight—and especially tight on the *Orient's* voyage to Egypt, when she carried nearly twice as many people as her normal crew of 1,100. The drawing shows Bonaparte in conference in the great cabin (*grande chambre*), just below the Admiral's day cabin (*salle de conseil*), his living quarters aboard ship. Vice-Admiral Brueys slept in the smaller captain's cabin. Other officers generally slept in tiny cabins off the wardroom; midshipmen were packed into the gunrooms and the open area just forward (*salle de garde*). The rest of the crew slept in hammocks slung up over the guns on the lower decks. For toilets—or heads (*poulaines*)—the seamen used seats slung out over the water at the ship's bow; officers had similar, but more private arrangements.

Below the gun decks and the water line, in the vast, dark spaces of the hold (*cale*), were the ship's storage areas. Here were kept salt beef and pork, biscuit, fresh water, and ample supplies of wine. Here also was stored the vast amount of gunpowder that would eventually send the *Orient* to her fiery death.

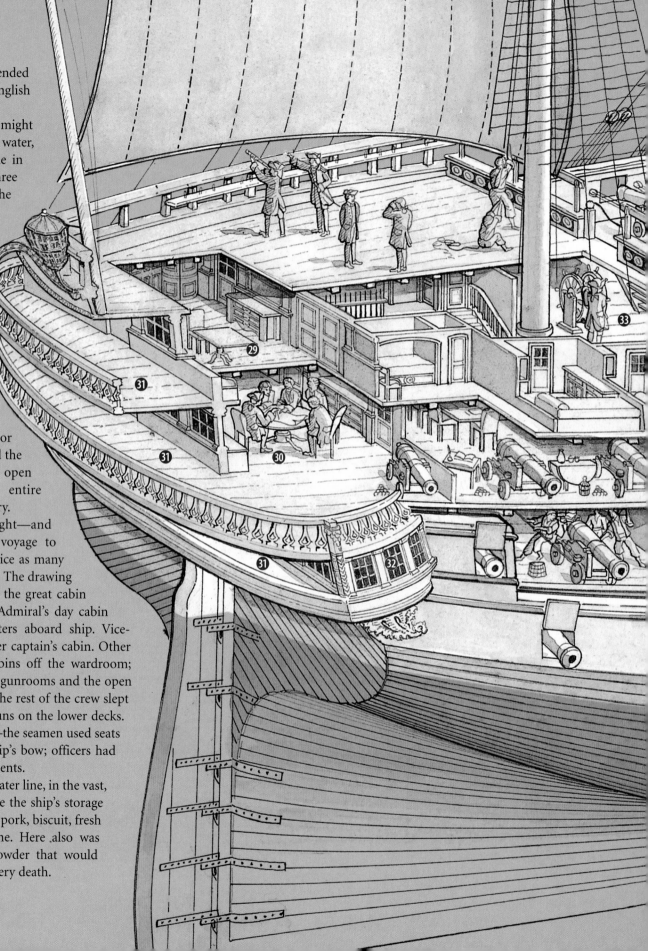

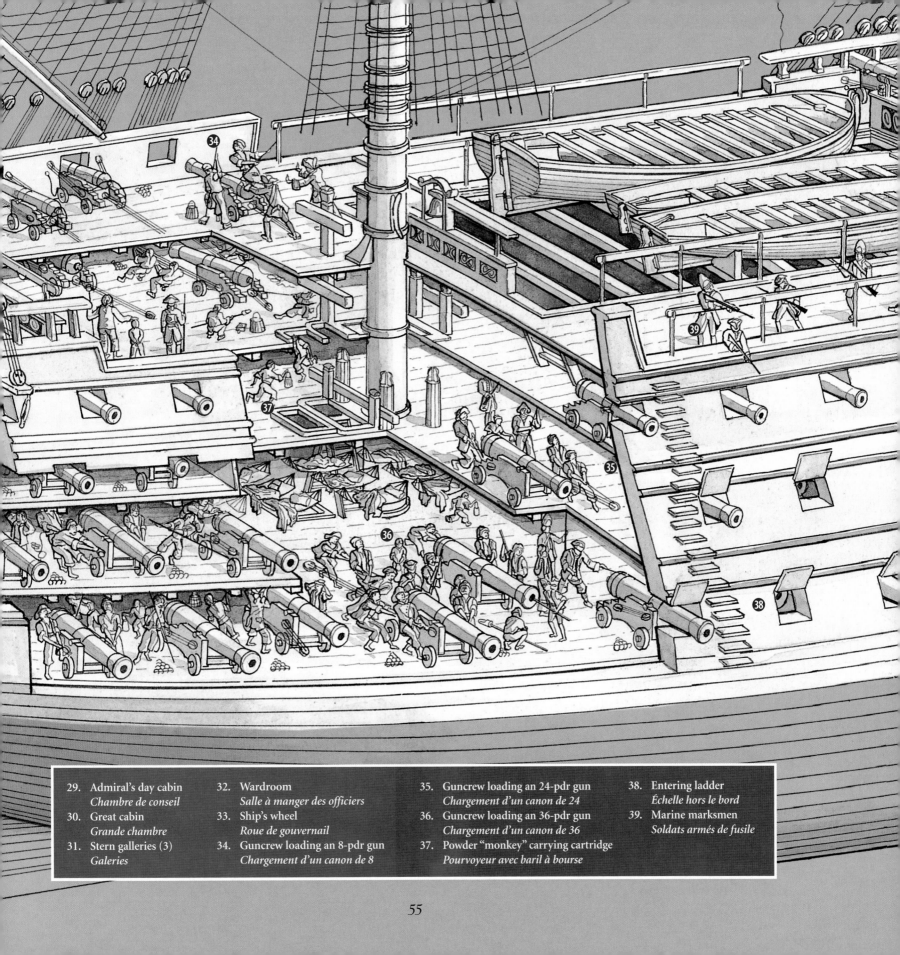

29.	Admiral's day cabin *Chambre de conseil*	32.	Wardroom *Salle à manger des officiers*	35.	Guncrew loading an 24-pdr gun *Chargement d'un canon de 24*	38.	Entering ladder *Échelle hors le bord*
30.	Great cabin *Grande chambre*	33.	Ship's wheel *Roue de gouvernail*	36.	Guncrew loading an 36-pdr gun *Chargement d'un canon de 36*	39.	Marine marksmen *Soldats armés de fusile*
31.	Stern galleries (3) *Galeries*	34.	Guncrew loading an 8-pdr gun *Chargement d'un canon de 8*	37.	Powder "monkey" carrying cartridge *Pourvoyeur avec baril à bourse*		

pieces of artillery and its vehicles; 45,000 tons of gunpowder; 12,000 tons of lead; and enough food, water, and brandy (in theory) for two months. "Here I am, transformed into an argonaut," said the irrepressible Monge, leaving Civitavecchia. "This is another one of those miracles produced by our new Jason."

Although the English fleet had been absent from the Mediterranean for several years, there were conflicting reports of sightings; one of Brueys's ships, sent out to reconnoiter, had been chased by three British ships of the line. Brueys therefore charted the safest course he could find. He led the Marseilles and Toulon convoys along the Mediterranean coast to the Gulf of Genoa, where General d'Hilliers's division joined him on May 21. Swinging sharply south-southeast, then southward along the Corsican coast, he picked up Vaubois's division on May 27; the next day the fleet sighted Desaix's convoy from Civitavecchia. "Here we are, all united for the first time, sailing now toward our destination," Bonaparte wrote to the Directory in Paris. That first destination was the island of Malta.

*　*　*

Malta's position in the center of the Mediterranean was not the sole reason for its attractiveness to

A 1775 lithograph shows the main gate and formidable defenses of Valletta, the Knights Hospitalers' fortress-capital on Malta. Three forts, thousands of yards of battlements, and more than nine hundred cannons guarded the entrance to Valetta's harbor. The artillery was antique, however, and the defending force for the city amounted to only 1,772 men.

Bonaparte: great wealth was to be had there. This was the home and headquarters of the venerable Order of the Knights Hospitalers of Saint John of Jerusalem, established during the Crusades in 1113 A.D. to protect European pilgrims and endowed with the lands and riches of every pious lord of Christendom.

The knightly order's path to the island had been roundabout. In the Holy Land the first knights had fortified themselves in the magnificent Belvoir Castle, "set among the stars like an eagle's nest," an Arab adversary remarked. After an eighteen-month siege, Belvoir fell to the Turks, and the knights, still a potent fighting force, moved to the island of Rhodes. From there they continued to battle Islam—now using galleys at sea—until defeat in 1522. By 1530 they were lords of Malta. In that century their formidable defenses and armaments were strong enough to withstand even Suleiman the Magnificent, who besieged the island for 233 days, only to withdraw, leaving behind thirty thousand dead Turkish troops.

By the late eighteenth century the situation had changed, although this might not have been evident to enemies approaching by sea. The knights' city, Valletta, set on a tongue of land amid a group of harbors, bristled with towering fortifications. The outermost was Fort St. Elmo; behind it stood the high-walled city; behind the city, on the landward side, were formidable ranks of bastions. Harbors to the east and north were similarly defended: "Malta has this advantage over all the other ports . . . that the whole harbor is covered by its wonderful fortifications," a British admiral would later observe. "At Malta all the arsenals, hospitals, storehouses, etc., are on a grand scale." From the sea the lofty battlements seemed as impregnable to Europeans as they had been to the Turks.

The once-great order that ruled the island, however, was in decline. The Crusades were long over; the old European aristocracies who had supplied younger sons as warrior monks were less enthusiastic. In fact, the order now recruited primarily from France; about two-thirds of the knights were French, and many were elderly. The subject Maltese regarded them with jaundiced eyes. The warriors themselves had not fought a battle since 1718, and then they had failed.

Bonaparte had already sent spies (with bribes) to the island. They discovered that it had a force of about three thousand men, supposedly backed by a native militia of ten thousand. The militia, untrained and unenthusiastic, were not likely to turn out for the knights, especially against a French revolutionary force that promised liberation. As for the fortifications, the walls remained mighty, but few of the nine hundred cannons had been fired within living memory.

The conquest looked like a walkover to Bonaparte, and it was. On June 9 the Maltese awoke to find themselves confronting a "floating forest" of masts and sail. The French sent in a request demanding that all their ships be allowed to enter the harbors to take on water. The grand master, a Prussian aristocrat named Hompesch, refused, pointing out that his order's regulations forbade navies at war with Christian countries to send in more than four ships at a time.

The leader of the French expedition now had a paper excuse for invasion. "The Commander in Chief, Bonaparte, is most indignant that you will not grant such permission," his next message began, concluding that "General Bonaparte is resolved to obtain by force what which ought to have been accorded him by virtue of the principles of hospitality, the fundamental rule of your order."

On the morning of June 10, the French attack began, directed not at the high walls of Valletta but at weaker defenses to the west of the city, on the eastern side of the island, and at the small neighboring islet of Gozo. Although the Maltese actually put up a defense—inaccurate firing from the battlements at Valletta and a charge by the four galleys of the Maltese navy (each armed with a three-pound gun), as well as fierce fire from smaller forts—their cause was clearly doomed. The knights were too few to man the guns and ramparts, and they had no hope of reinforcement, being unaware that a British fleet was then off the coast of Italy.

In this tinted engraving, Bonaparte's fleet bombards Malta. Victory was a forgone conclusion: the naval opposition consisted of only a few galleys, the knights' defense was weak, and on June 11, 1798— after less than a day's battle—the Knights Hospitalers sued for peace.

In any case, their emotions were conflicted. The French knights were divided between their loyalty to the order and that to their homeland, however much it had changed. The Maltese themselves were pragmatic: "I fear very much that the Grand Master knows not what he is doing," said a lawyer acting as a sentinel. "They are firing away; but to what purpose? It can only alarm women and children." And, more to the point, he added, "What? Sacrifice ourselves for a handful of degenerate and panic-stricken knights, who do not know how to defend, govern or command us!"

The results were as Bonaparte expected. On the morning of June 12, the knights asked for a truce. That evening they agreed to give up the island. Their conquerors promised the grand master help in finding a petty principality to rule and offered to make arrangements with their home governments for all knights. None of these promises was kept.

Always impatient and now alert to the presence of an English fleet in the Mediterranean, Bonaparte stayed less than a week on Malta. He spent it issuing dispatches falsely claiming that his attack had been provoked because the knights had supported French émigrés and the Spanish and British while denying help to the republic. He also freed the knights' galley slaves and reorganized the government, hospitals, churches, and monasteries.

This last activity did not endear the French to the devoutly Catholic Maltese. The faithful were to be even less pleased when the French

A contemporary engraving shows Bonaparte in the launch boat on his way to Malta after the quick victory. He went on land to claim his prize, then returned to the Orient *and continued to issue orders from on board until setting sail for Egypt on June 19.*

removed not only the fabled fortune of the knights from the grand master's palace and its Church of St. Anthony, but also precious art, donated by believers over the centuries and housed in Malta's palaces and churches—gold; silver plate; bejeweled reliquaries, book bindings, and crucifixes; bronze and ivory statuary; models of ships in silver; rare silk altar cloths from China. Lying like a bulletin, Bonaparte told the Directory that the value of the loot was in the range of a million francs. The figure actually was nearer 7 million, and most of it apparently went into the hold of the *Orient*.

With this booty in hand, plus firewood, fresh water, vegetables, and four hundred Maltese sheep, the French were ready to sail. Stationing a garrison of three thousand men on the island, they left Malta for Egypt on June 19.

* * *

Brueys pursued his careful path east toward Crete and then south, hurried along by a frigate's sighting of what it said were sixteen British ships heading down the coast of Italy. All Brueys heard of them was the gunfire on the night of June 22; after that, he had clear sailing. Along the southern coast of Crete, he

picked up the northerly wind, the *meltemi*, and began to make good speed for Alexandria—60 to 80 miles a day. On June 27 Napoleon sent the swift little frigate *Junon* ahead of the fleet to reconnoiter and contact the French consul.

The news that the *Junon* brought back to the fleet as it neared Alexandria on June 30 set everyone's nerves on edge. A British fleet of fourteen ships had come and gone from the port; the Egyptians, having heard of the conquest of Malta, were manning their forts. The wild Bedouin armies of their deserts were gathering.

Bonaparte decided to land his forces with the greatest speed. From the sea the walls of Alexandria looked well fortified. He therefore chose to disembark his troops 7 miles away, at Marabout Bay. It had a long beach and seemed reasonably sheltered.

The sandbars protecting the beach, however, meant shallow water, which prevented even the transports from anchoring closer than a mile and a half away from land; to protect the mass of ships and men, Brueys's fleet, whose ships had deeper drafts, anchored in a battle line another mile out from the transports. The troops would have to toil ashore in small ships' boats—longboats, cutters, barges, and even a galley brought from Malta. And they would have to do

A sixteenth-century ceremonial dagger was among the many prizes Bonaparte received at Malta. The dagger's hilt is encrusted with gold;

its sheath, adorned with the bees Bonaparte used as his symbol, was made in the nineteenth century.

A contemporary engraving depicts Bonaparte's landing in Egypt on July 1, 1798. Driven by his destiny, as he said, and fearing that a British fleet might appear to challenge him, Bonaparte insisted his army disembark in the midst of a howling gale over uncharted reefs.

this in heavy seas, with night falling.

Brueys sensibly advised his commander to delay the landing. "Admiral, we have no time to lose," Bonaparte replied. "Fortune has given me three days; if I do not profit from it, we are lost." In the gathering darkness, therefore, hundreds of small boats fought their way to shore.

It was chaos. Bonaparte's estimate (certainly an underestimate) was that twenty soldiers drowned. Just after midnight, however, the general and his commanders reviewed a ragged formation of about five thousand soaking, seasick men. Early the next morning, leaving a guard at the beachhead, Bonaparte marched his army along the sand toward the walls of the city.

Fortunately for the French, Alexandria's fortifications had been neglected for decades. The beys who led the Mamelukes claimed that maintaining them would be seen by their Ottoman overlords as a threat. A contemporary Arab observer dryly remarked that this excuse was "as frail as a spider's web." Reviewing the

course of events, he added that "Alexandria and its towers had once been extremely well built and fortified with an excellent wall surrounding her; a wall which had been maintained by former generations. Three hundred and sixty towers were incorporated into this wall, corresponding to the days of the year. Every tower had its own ammunition depot, supplies, and garrison. All these were neglected until nothing remained while the wall and its towers fell into ruin, until in some places the walls became level with the ground."

Given these conditions, the five thousand French, even without their not-yet-landed artillery, took the city with ease and within the day. Their casualties, variously reported, were fifteen to forty killed and sixty to one hundred wounded, among them General Kléber, who was shot in the head but would continue to function for months.

Bonaparte then issued an Arabic proclamation intending to divide the Egyptians from their Mameluke and Turkish rulers: "For too long this rabble of slaves

THE EGYPTIAN VIEWPOINT

How does it feel to be invaded by infidels? The contemporary Ottoman historian Abd al-Rahman Al-Jabarti gave the answer: Not good.

Al-Jabarti reported that the French advanced on Alexandria "like a swarm of locusts." He read Bonaparte's announcement of friendship to Islam carefully and commented that a man who boasted of the destruction of the Papal See belonged to a people who are "opposed to both Christians and Muslims, and do not hold fast to any religion."

This skepticism increased with the occupation of Cairo, although Al-Jabarti was impressed by the French army's courage. It was only too clear from looting and taxation that the French were dedicated to one purpose only: "robbing people of their money by devious means and despoiling them of their real estate, inherited property, and the like."

The invaders—with the possible exception of members of the Egyptian Institute—were disgusting savages. The historian, observing Bonaparte's headquarters, commented, "The French entered it [headquarters], stepping on the carpets with their shoes and sandals . . . since they never take off their shoes with which they tread upon filth, not even when they sleep! Among their repulsive habits also is their practice of spitting and blowing their noses upon the furnishings."

Considering French behavior, it is not surprising that Al-Jabarti took some satisfaction in their defeat by Nelson. He provided a clear assessment of France's aggression in Europe, its attempt to conquer the British through Egypt, and the defeat itself, which occurred, he remarked, because "the English are known for their strength and valor in sea battles, while the French are just the opposite."

A nineteenth-century engraving by Dutertre shows a sheik of Cairo.

bought in Georgia and Caucasia have tyrannized over the most beautiful part of the world, but God, from whom all depends, has ordered that their empire shall cease." He went on to declare that under his rule Egyptians would hold office and that the French were true friends of the Muslims. This message was received by literate Egyptians with contempt for its grammar and skepticism for its promises.

The French army was skeptical as well: "These are the six acres they promised us," said one soldier, surveying the dusty streets, crumbling walls, and empty shores of the port. The troops were sullen. Partly to keep them under control, Bonaparte began marching separate divisions inland within two days. These took Rosetta and Dmanhour, thus securing the western Nile delta. Reuniting at Rahmaniya on the Nile, they began the march south toward Cairo.

The march was agony, through a landscape from evil dreams. Just outside Alexandria's walls the desert began, first sandy hills flecked with palms, then endless miles of rolling dunes littered with the rotting carcasses or bones of camels, horses, and cattle. Those who looked toward the horizon always saw great stretches of water with trees reflected in it and moving gray vapor overhead. The promising scene always receded: it was only the familiar mirage of the desert.

Bonaparte's troops were expected to live off the land, as in European campaigns, but in this land there was nothing to eat. The constant mirage was perhaps the worst torment because there was also nothing to drink. What wells the men found were filled in or poisoned. During the early part of the nineteen-day march to

Cairo, thirst, hunger, heatstroke, and lightning attacks by Bedouins killed hundreds of men. When the army arrived at the fertile fields and villages in the interior, they fell savagely upon the people they were supposed to be liberating. Despite Bonaparte's orders, they devastated the countryside. The wails of women followed them as they marched.

They had no choice but to go on, and on July 21 at Embaben—a town on the outskirts of Cairo and within sight of the Great Pyramid—they met the Mamelukes. Under the command of two resourceful leaders, Ibrahim Bey and Murad Bey, were six thousand cavalrymen in jeweled regalia, armed with javelins, sabers, bows, and muskets, each supported by a retinue of peasants. They were joined by eight thousand Bedouins.

The French force consisted of five divisions totaling twenty-five thousand men. They formed into impenetrable squares bristling with bayonets to repel the Mameluke charges. The roar of their gunfire and the pounding of the Mamelukes' horses could be heard in Cairo. The Battle of the Pyramids was simply slaughter, and it was over within an hour. Egyptian losses were put

at twenty-five hundred, French at one hundred. While French soldiers scavenged among the dead bodies, Murad Bey's cavalry retreated south toward Gaza, and Ibrahim Bey's east into the desert. Both would fight another day. Perhaps Bonaparte counted his conquest of Egypt as nearly complete. If so, he was sadly mistaken.

*   *   *

On the coast Vice Admiral Brueys was deeply uneasy, but he was not the man to challenge his commander. The admiral was a loyal, honorable, unimaginative son of the aristocracy, trained from the age of thirteen in the hierarchies of the navy. Through the vicissitudes of the Revolution, he remained a patriot. Moreover, he admired Bonaparte, whose orders he did his best to implement. Even though his understanding of warfare at sea was infinitely superior to Bonaparte's, he could not withstand the general's sheer willpower. Thus, when Bonaparte insisted on the difficult and dangerous landing at Marabout, he had acquiesced, even though he deplored the decision.

When ordered by dispatch from Cairo to take his fighting fleet into Alexandria's Old Harbor for the purpose of unloading the remaining troops and artillery ("if the winds slacken and the channel is deep enough," wrote Bonaparte), the admiral began the complicated soundings that would determine whether this was practicable. Within days he decided that it was not. Three channels led into the harbor, the best no more than 30 feet at its minimum depth. This was adequate for the transports, which took shelter there, but it was danger-

ous for the much larger ships of the line, with their deeper drafts. Brueys therefore completed the unloading at Aboukir Bay, nine miles east of Alexandria.

This done, the defense of the fleet remained a question discussed in a series of dispatches carried by messengers between Alexandria and Cairo. It seemed unlikely that the British would retrace their path to Alexandria, but it would have been madness not to prepare for them. Bonaparte still wanted his ships in Alexandria's Old Harbor, where they would theoretically be protected by forts and land batteries. Given the channel depths, taking them in was just possible; with calm seas and fair winds, the great vessels might enter the harbor at the rate of two each day. As Brueys dutifully pointed out, however, they could emerge only at the same rate. A single British ship could blockade the entire fleet.

Brueys's own idea was to take his fleet to Corfu, placing himself at the British rear and cutting their lines of communication should they return for an attack on Alexandria. Bonaparte would have none of this. He wanted the fleet at his disposal, ready to do his bidding, whatever that might be. He might, for instance, want Brueys available to import more convoys of troops and supplies. On the other hand, after a few Egyptian victories he might wish to return to France and prepare an invasion of Britain itself. If safe harbor could not be made in the Old Harbor, he wrote to his naval commander, then Brueys might anchor in Aboukir Bay, the only other option along that shallow, difficult coast. The admiral would be permitted to withdraw from there "only if the enemy appears with a very superior force."

A popular French cartoon conveys the tremendous impact of Bonaparte's exotic Egyptian expedition. He is shown crowned by Renown and by Glory.

With these orders, Brueys moved his fleet from stations off Alexandria to Aboukir on July 7.

The bay was not without defensive advantages. A 30-mile-long curve ending at one of the two mouths of the Nile, it had been carved by millennia of silting into a maze of channels and shoals, a natural trap for ships unfamiliar with the soundings. At its western end was a fort provided by the French with twenty guns and fifty men. Below this lay a small island, walled by shoals on the seaward side, and a further series of rocks and shoals that narrowed the mouth of the bay. No warship could anchor within a mile and a half of this island, well out of range of artillery; nevertheless, the army engineers equipped it with two mortars and, for its own defense, a number of six-pounder guns.

In the weeks that followed, while Brueys moved his ships into the best defensive positions he could devise,

he was having to cope with a more immediately serious problem. The navy had provisioned his fleet, but Bonaparte had taken these supplies to feed his troops. The Egyptians would sell food only for cash, and despite his treasurer's pleas, Bonaparte would not release it. By mid-July, one captain noted, the situation was growing desperate. Word reached Brueys on July 24 that five or six vessels loaded with emergency food were being sent down the Nile; he was deeply grateful. As he said, his men, wracked with dysentery, were "truly on the verge of dying of hunger and thirst." While they waited for relief, large parties foraged on the barren shore, fending off Bedouin attacks.

Just off the shore shoals—close enough so that no enemy should be able to slip behind his lines, and perhaps close enough to the fort to permit some protection—Brueys positioned his ships in a 2-mile-long curving line stretching from the northwest to the southeast. The vessels were spaced about 200 yards apart and at a distance from the shoals that allowed them to swing safely when anchored only from the stern.

If the British should reappear—and no one could imagine where they might be—it would probably be from the west, Brueys reasoned. A conventional man himself, he expected a conventional attack on his center and his rear. He therefore placed the mighty 124-gun *Orient* at the very center of the line, flanked by the 80-gun *Franklin* and *Tonnant*. From the *Tonnant* his powerful rear lay in line to the southeast—the *Heureux, Mercure, Guillaume Tell, Généreux,* and *Timoléon*, all of them 74s except for the 80-gun *Guillaume Tell*. His van—the *Peuple Souverain, Aquilon, Spartiate, Conquérant,* and *Guerrier*—lay northwest of the *Franklin*. These ships were 74s as well, but the *Conquérant* was old, weakened in structure, and only lightly armed. She had been used,

To demonstrate that the disease ravishing his troops at Jaffa was not the bubonic plague, Napoleon touched a victim's bubo, an incident memorialized in the 1800 painting by Antoine-Jean Gros. Bonaparte was wrong. Hundreds of soldiers died.

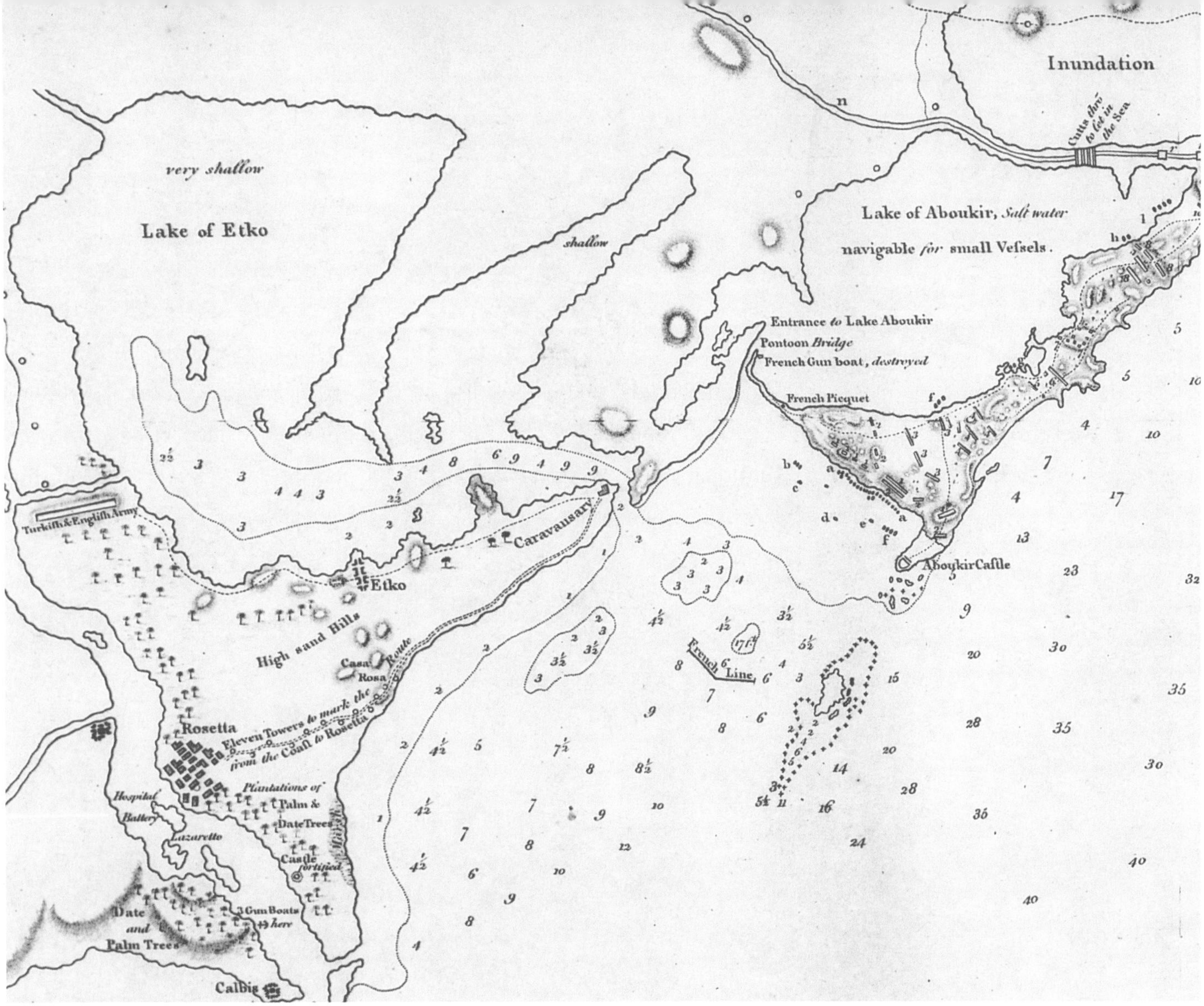
Inundation
very shallow
Lake of Etko
shallow
Lake of Aboukir, Salt water
navigable for small Vessels.
Entrance to Lake Aboukir
Pontoon Bridge
French Gun boat, destroyed
French Picquet
Aboukir Castle
Turkish & English Army
Caravansary
Etko
High sand Hills
Casa Rosa
Route
Rosetta
Eleven Towers to mark the Route from the Coast to Rosetta
Plantations of Palm & Date Trees
Hospital Battery
Lazaretto
Castle fortified
Date and Palm Trees
3 Gun Boats here
Calbig
French Line

A chart of the Alexandria area published by the British Admiralty in 1801 clearly shows the dilemma of Vice Admiral Brueys in anchoring his fleet safely. Aboukir Bay (center) is open to the sea and cluttered with dangerous shoals.

in fact, primarily as a transport. Perhaps because he was desperately short of manpower, perhaps because he really believed the British would not reappear, Brueys kept his frigates with the fleet, not on patrol outside the bay.

The survival of the fleet, Brueys knew, depended on the wind, highly variable in the Mediterranean. When it blew from the southwest, he was safe, because a southwest wind would force an adversary on a long tack toward him, all the time exposed to his broadsides. When it blew from the west, the adversary, once past the shoals guarding the bay, could attack the fleet at any point along the line. If the wind should blow from the northwest, the enemy would have it broad on their beams and be able to move down the line as they wished.

Under the brutal sun of late July, the French ships lay at anchor in the bright bay, thousands of their men milling about on shore in search of food and water. On July 26 Brueys had made a final appeal for supplies to Napoleon. “Without food or naval repairs, the fleet is now paralyzed,” he wrote. “We are floating between hope and despair.”

Nelson and his shipmates board the San Nicolás during the Battle of Cape St. Vincent.

Inset: Horatio Nelson was an eighteen-year-old lieutenant when this John Rigaud portrait was begun. When the painting was finished on Nelson's return to England from the West Indies in 1780, the artist was obliged to add a captain's insignia to young Nelson's sleeve.

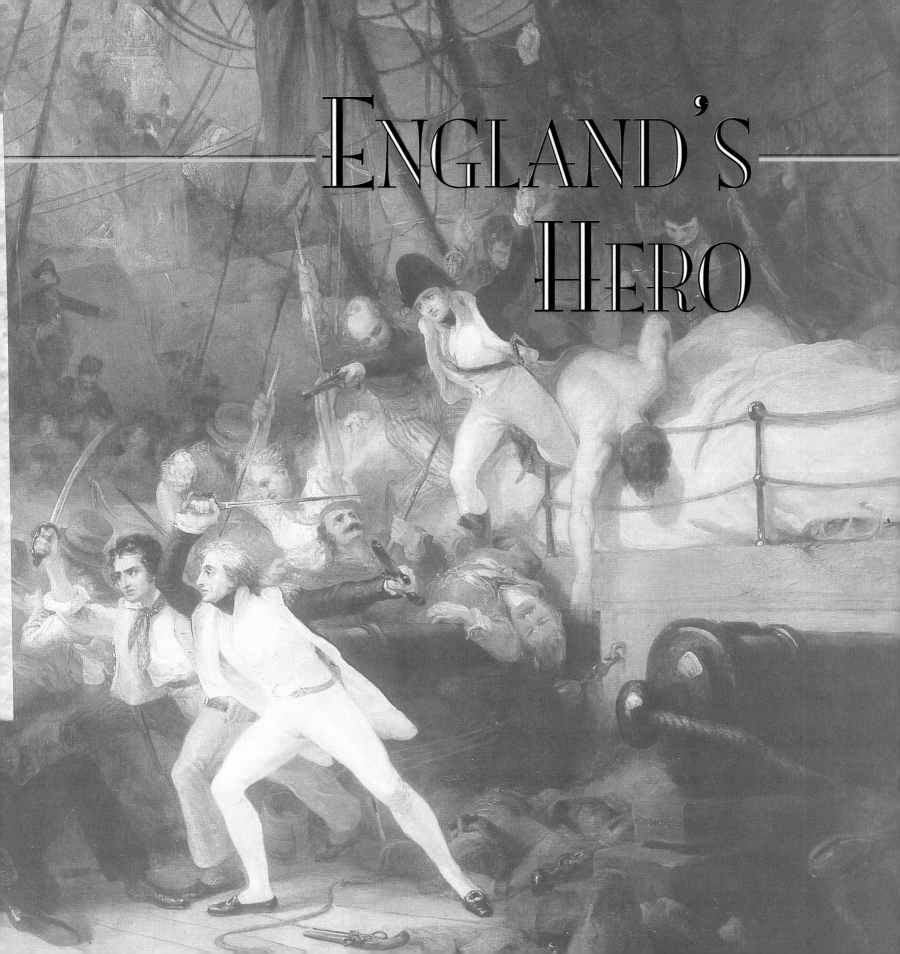

England's
Hero

NCERTAINTY WAS ANATHEMA to Horatio Nelson's nature. Impatient with subtleties and not overly given to introspection, he was happiest when reality arranged itself in stark and tidy blacks and whites. That was perhaps one reason he took such joy in battle, that least gray of circumstances, wherein one did one's duty, fought hard, won or lost, lived or died. Goals were clear-cut in battle, and outcomes tended to be unequivocal. Fighting, Nelson was at his best; no fear or doubt could assail him.

Roistering English sailors take leave of land's pleasures as they set out to sea from Portsmouth in this painting by illustrator Thomas Rowlandson. Bracketing the scene are two establishments much frequented by seamen ashore, a tavern and a moneylender.

Now, though, there was no battle—only the relentless, wearing search for one as his fleet crisscrossed the Mediterranean in pursuit of Bonaparte's armada. Nothing at Egypt. Nothing at Syria. Sailing east again toward Italy, the admiral retired early each night to his comfortable sleeping cabin, but he did not stay there. He napped only fitfully, spending most of the dark hours walking the *Vanguard*'s quarterdeck, pacing for miles, silent and deep within himself. Several of his officers thought him near exhaustion, and he probably was. This was a most uncertain time: anxiety was ever present, and doubt gnawed deep.

Nelson's childhood home, the parsonage at Burnham Thorpe, consisted of two large cottages joined together. The boy holding the flag in the foreground of this Francis Pocock painting is believed to be young Nelson.

At least the horizon was familiar; he knew the Mediterranean well. He had tasted his first glory here, had commanded his first ship of the line on these sapphire waters, and had fought on their shores. He knew this southern sea's capricious weather, its sunlit calms and ship-mauling storms. But what he did not know—and this was all that mattered at present—was what part of it sheltered his enemy.

Never had the Mediterranean seemed so overwhelmingly vast, so hostile, so far from home.

*   *   *

The sea that had helped shape Nelson was far more harsh and less lovely, but it was nevertheless a childhood friend. He was born about 5 miles inland from the North Sea, that chilly arm of the Atlantic that gouges into England's eastern coast. The island's coldest winds sweep directly from the Arctic across its silver waters and onto the flat salt marshes that fringe Norfolk, informing the local character. The people there, many descended from Viking raiders, tend to be taciturn, stoical, and self-reliant.

Burnham Thorpe, where Nelson was born on September 29, 1758, is one of several villages just inside the border where marshes give way to flat or gently rolling farmland, the richest in England. Ubiquitous hedgerows segmented the land in Nelson's day, hedges mounded with wind-whipped snow in winter, spangled in spring and summer with blackthorn blossoms and wild rose as the fields between them turned gold with wheat and barley or blue with flowering flax. The homes and shops and pubs there were built of plaster or black flint, sturdy structures that survived both time and weather. Far more imposing were East Anglia's churches, so numerous that every plot of Norfolk ground afforded a view of a church tower. In the mid-eighteenth century, one of these edifices, Burnham Thorpe's parish church of All Saints, was presided over by the Reverend Edmund Nelson, Horatio's father.

The Reverend Mr. Nelson was a quiet, kindly man,

married to Catherine Suckling, a woman who bore him eleven children, eight surviving past infancy. The last was only nine months old when Catherine died in 1767. Horatio, called Young Horace by the family, was nine at the time.

Faced with rearing his brood alone, Edmund Nelson tempered affection with discipline, for he meant to give his offspring, above all, a moral compass that pointed true north. He sought to instill reverence for duty toward God, king, and country, and he insisted on decorum. At table the soldier-straight spines of his children made no contact with

Nelson's parents, the Reverend Edmund Nelson and his wife, Catherine, were sober, respectable country folk. Horatio Nelson's clearest memory of his well-born mother was her hatred of the French.

the backs of their chairs. The weak-eyed among them were denied the frivolity of spectacles; if God had intended everyone to have perfect vision, he would have made it so. Edmund had no patience with vanity or the world's diversions. "Variety," he once said, "the Great Idoll, has no shrine here."

Indeed, his parsonage was far too sober and simple to accommodate any such shrine, but it was a pleasant place nonetheless, an L-shaped, two-story house surrounded by 30 acres of lawns and fields. There young Horace passed a happy, unremarkable childhood and seemed an unremarkable boy—small, thin, and constitutionally frail. He was, however, uncommonly fearless and persistent at times, whether in mischief or dead earnest. (He once stole some pears from a headmaster's

garden, explaining that he "only took them because every other boy was afraid." On another occasion he and his older brother William were riding their ponies through deep snow on their way to catch a coach to school, under their father's orders to return home only if the way was clearly impassable. William thought it was, but Horatio insisted they press on. "Remember, brother," he said, "it was left to our honour.")

Despite such precocious self-possession, young Horace appeared destined for no great deeds. His schooling was basic: at home and at nearby private academies, he learned the requisites—his figures, his Bible, his Shakespeare, his Milton—but no career path suggested itself. Except, perhaps, the sea. During trips to coastal villages, he found that he liked the salt smell of it, liked watching the ships and learning to recognize their various types by size and sail, masts and rigging. Moreover, the calling suited a boy of his prospects. The army's officer corps generally drew from the aristocracy, the navy's from the gentry and the rising middle class. And Horatio, like countless other English boys, must have found the notion of life at sea romantic. The navy was the nation's pride, the source of her wealth and protector of her shores, and its successful officers were celebrated. The best of this dashing breed might sail to peerages or riches or both. (Or to disgrace and an early death, but what boy was apt to dwell on that?) In any case, the idea of a naval career remained latent until one day, when Horatio was twelve, history took him in hand.

England and Spain, disputing possession of the distant Falkland Islands, appeared on the verge of war. Ships of the Royal Navy mothballed after the Seven Years War were recommissioned, among them the 64-gun *Raisonnable*, captured from the French twelve years earlier. Horatio read about it in the *Norfolk Chronicle*, which also reported that the *Raisonnable* would be commanded by Captain Maurice Suckling, who happened to be his uncle.

Edmund Nelson was impecunious, but he was not without connections. His family had once owned considerable land, and his wife—Maurice Suckling's sister—had been the great-niece of Sir Robert Walpole, the first earl of Orford and for twenty-seven years King George II's prime minister. (The grand Walpoles paid little attention to the lowly Nelsons; nevertheless, the parson was proud of the kinship.) In Nelson's day, using family ties to further careers was in no way scorned;

anyone who had connections used them, and he who did otherwise was deemed eccentric or a fool. So it was that Horatio asked his father to petition Uncle Maurice to take him to sea, and Suckling happily obliged. "What has poor Horace done, who is so weak, that he, above all the rest, should be sent to rough it out at sea?" the captain wrote in a jocular note to the father. "But let him come; and the first time we go into action a cannon-ball may knock off his head and provide for him at once."

On his first day in His Majesty's Navy, midshipman Nelson was at sea only metaphorically. Standing dockside in the winter wind at the port of Chatham early in 1771, the shivering, undersized boy could see the *Raisonnable* resting at anchor in the Medway River's broad estuary, but he had no idea how to reach her. At last a kindly officer took pity and secured a boat to ferry him to his new home.

It was an inauspicious introduction to a world where variety, that old Idoll, certainly had a toehold, at least in the bewildering assortment of skills and procedures and customs that an apprentice officer had to master if he ever hoped to command the floating kingdom that was a British ship of the line.

*   *   *

It was said that a bright, enterprising midshipman could learn most of what he needed to know about shipboard life in a few months' time. This was fortunate for Horatio Nelson, who was aboard the *Raisonnable* barely five months before she was once again decommissioned. Spain had backed off her claim to the Falklands,

MAURICE SUCKLING.
CAPTAIN . R.N.
AFTER BARDWELL . 1764.
DIED . 1778 .

Captain Maurice Suckling, Nelson's maternal uncle, introduced the boy to the Royal Navy and nurtured his early career. Suckling later rose to be comptroller of the navy.

THE BRITISH MIDSHIPMAN: APPRENTICESHIP AT SEA

It would not have taken Midshipman Horatio Nelson long to learn that life aboard ship—at least below decks—was harsh, cramped, uncomfortable, malodorous, and exhausting.

MEALS ON BOARD

Midshipmen—as many as twenty aboard a large warship—were berthed on the lowest deck, the dank and airless orlop, packed into a room no larger than 10 by 18 feet. They also ate below decks, not with the well-fed officers, and the fare, while hearty enough, was sometimes revolting, at least by modern standards. Breakfast was generally burgoo, a watery oatmeal, capped off with "coffee" made of hot water and burned biscuit—while the biscuits lasted. A ship was seldom long out of port before the biscuits filled with maggots, an occurrence so common that some sailors even developed a taste for them. They were "very cold when you eat them, like calf's foot jelly or blomonge," a midshipman reported to his parents. But the maggots eventually gave way to weevils, which caused the biscuits to crumble away altogether.

At the noon meal, the largest of the day, biscuits might be joined by salt beef or pork, pease pudding (porridge made of split peas), raisins, and on good days butter and cheese, usually rancid. Enterprising crewmen also caught and ate rats, fondly called "millers" because their forays into the flour stores left their fur powdered white. Dining was done between the guns on planks suspended from ropes attached to the deckheads. Alcohol helped lift the crew's spirits, its nature depending on where the ship saw service: beer in home waters, wine in the Mediterranean, and in the West Indies grog—watered-down rum, often enlivened with lemon juice to improve the taste and protect against scurvy.

Old hands liked to reminisce about the awfulness of shipboard food, of vermin-laden victuals and meat grown hard enough to sculpt. In fact, however, most captains supplied their men with fresh meat and vegetables whenever circumstances allowed, and a menu that included one hot meal a day was superior to what most sailors could have expected on land in a time when life among society's lower orders was unremittingly harsh. The smells below decks might have been enough to blunt the appetite: the stench of unwashed bodies, boiling salt meat, tar and tallow, and the excrement of chickens and livestock penned aft on the lower gun deck to provide fresh meat and fowl for the fortunate officers. Even so, the connection between decent nutrition and good health was understood in Nelson's day, and part of the British navy's success

A new midshipman gazes in dismay at the cramped and noisy life awaiting him below decks in the Royal Navy. In this sketch by Captain Frederick Marryat, once a midshipman himself, older midshipmen enjoy their rum and a fifer's tune while younger boys attend to chores or try to rest. At right (above) is a ship's biscuit that was hard enough to inscribe. It was given to a Miss Blacket of Berwick in 1784.

was attributable to its sailors being the best fed in the world.

STARTING FROM BELOW

Nelson was lucky to begin his career as a midshipman, entitled to the few perquisites of a junior officer. Boys as young as six sometimes went to sea as "powder monkeys," running gunpowder from the magazine to the gun crews during battle, and lads of eight or nine might be officers' servants who could not expect to become midshipmen until they were fifteen. The midshipman's main task was to assist lieutenants, spending hours on the quarterdeck, the exclusive preserve of the officers, doing the bidding of his superiors. Each noon he took sightings of the sun with the captain to determine the ship's position. In battle he supervised small fighting units, such as groups of guns. On larger vessels schooling—morning classes in

Above: Guilty of some minor infraction, a midshipman finds himself aloft for a form of punishment called "mastheading." He has lashed himself to the topgallant crosstrees and naps through the experience, a book at his side.
Right: The youthful officer in this Thomas Rowlandson aquatint wears the midshipman's formal uniform: a blue coat with a white patch on the collar, white breeches and hose, and a cocked hat.

A midshipman tries to hold his footing in heavy swells by bracing himself against a stanchion near the mainmast. It appears that one of his colleagues has been upended by loose cannonballs careening across the pitching deck.

navigation and mathematics with the ship's schoolmaster—was part of his daily routine.

Just as vital, however, was the education he got aloft and on the gun decks. To become a good officer, he had to learn all he could about seafaring from every other man on board—not just the captain and lieutenants, who were the head of the fighting ship, but also the crewmen, who were its heart and sinew. He might not concern himself overmuch with the duties of the captain of the head (the landsman who cleaned the toilets) or the Jack-in-the-Dust (who swept up the gun room). But a good midshipman studied the petty officers and warrant officers and the higher echelons among the "ratings."

THE MEN
Ratings were sailors assigned to various categories by a ship's first lieutenant at the beginning of a voyage. At the bottom of the scale were the powder monkeys and serving boys. Next came landsmen, at sea for the first time. Above them were ordinary seamen, who knew the basic shipboard duties, and most highly prized were the able seamen, experienced hands who were qualified for many tasks and could hope to become petty officers. All these lived among the guns, the warship's reason for being. They ate on the gun decks, and there they slept, their canvas hammocks slung from the deckheads and spaced scant inches apart.

Among the ratings were agile young sailors called topmen, at home on the highest yardarms, and lead men, expert in testing the water's depth. And even the lowliest landsman contributed the muscle needed to haul cables and hoist longboats and drag a 5-ton anchor out

of the seabed.

Petty officers, who held their posts at the pleasure of the captain, included foremen for various parts of the ship—the yeoman of the sheets, for instance, who oversaw the operation of the fore and aft sails, and the coxswain, who supervised the ship's small boats. There were also gunner's mates, who helped maintain the cannons; quartermasters, who steered the ship and supervised timekeeping; and—loathed by the rest of the crew—the bosun's mates, who administered floggings and other punishments. Like the ratings, the petty officers ate and slept on the lower gun decks.

Warrant officers were appointed by the Navy Board, although they could be demoted, or disrated, by their ship's captain. The most senior of these, considered fellow gentlemen by the commissioned officers, were allowed on the quarterdeck and enjoyed the same food and

accommodations as the lieutenants, who slept in tiny compartments in the ward room on an upper gun deck. The highest warrant officer was the ship's master, responsible for piloting and navigation. Other senior warrant officers included surgeons, whose chief skill was amputating battle-damaged limbs, and on the most prestigious ships, chaplains. Chaplains were always in short supply; apparently, most English clergymen were sensible enough to serve God on dry land. The purser, the ship's accountant, who also sold clothing, tobacco, and a few other necessities and little luxuries to the crew, rounded out the senior group. Lower in status among the warrants were the gunner, the master's and surgeon's mates, the schoolmaster, and the bosun.

Ship's artificers often had warrant officer status and were vital on a man-of-war. There were sailmakers and ropemakers, armorers who saw to the upkeep of all metalwork, caulkers who

In spite of the punishments that might follow a drunken spree, merriment often broke the tedium of the day.

Seamen scrub the deck under the watchful eye of a lieutenant while in the background a midshipmen brings another lieutenant a morning cup of tea.

kept the hulls watertight. Most valued were the ship's carpenter and his mates, whose skill could determine a vessel's very survival. These were the men who fitted out a ship before she ever sailed and who at sea could rebuild a storm-damaged mast or patch a hull holed by a cannonball.

THE SHIP'S ROUTINE

The nautical day began officially at noon, but for most hands it started at 4 a.m. with the shrill cry of the bosun's pipe and his call of "All hands!" With that, the bosun's mates began walking the lower decks, flicking at any filled hammock with knotted ropes called "starters." Thus encouraged, the seamen quickly dressed and then lashed their hammocks into cylinders preparatory to having them "piped up"—stored in netting around the upper deck's bulwarks. (In battle the hammocks gave some protection against small projectiles and were also useful as life preservers.) Crewmen then began washing the decks and smoothing away splinters with sandstone scrapers called holystones because they were about the size of prayerbooks. The upper decks would be brushed and swabbed dry by 6 a.m., when a second shriek of the bosun's pipe signaled breakfast.

Labor at sea was a round-the-clock enterprise that required the division of the crew into two watches, the starboard and larboard. There were seven work shifts, also called watches. These were supervised by lieutenants and lasted four hours each, except for two dogwatches of two hours each between 4 p.m. and 8 p.m. A sandglass measured the half hours, and each time the glass was turned, a bell sounded. Eight bells denoted the end of a watch, at which time the ship's speed and course were logged.

The odd number of watches meant that night duty was fairly shared—the larboard watch beginning work at midnight one night, the starboard the next—but it also meant that crewmen rarely had more than four hours of sleep one night and seven hours the next. Fatigue was chronic.

Throughout the day there were drills—sail drills and fire drills, boat-lowering drills and the all-important gun drills, wherein the men practiced running the cannons in and out of the gun ports and sometimes firing them.

Shortly after supper the men were called to quarters. All hands sped to their battle stations, and the cannons were cast loose. Midshipmen and lieutenants inspected the divisions they supervised, then reported to the first lieutenant, who in turn informed the captain, if all was well, "All present and sober, sir, if you please." Thereafter, if the captain failed to order any more drills, the hammocks were piped down, and the men not on watch retired for the night or amused themselves as best they could, perhaps by playing cards or swapping tales or eliciting a tune from the ship's fiddler or fifer.

So went the course of a normal day. But sooner or later every ship of the line justified her existence by going into battle. Then all routine fled on the wind, and the crewmen, directed by their officers, merely fought—until they won or lost or (rarely) surrendered, or until they were maimed or killed. Usually they did win, and survivors were able to celebrate the fact that, however hard their lives, they were part of the greatest navy to sail the oceans of the earth.

and the war threat was over.

Maurice Suckling then got his nephew a berth on a merchant ship bound for the West Indies, and Nelson crossed the Atlantic twice, suffering from seasickness and acquiring from his shipmates an attitude that nearly aborted his nascent naval career. Merchant seaman, who were often impressed into the navy, generally hated it for its hard discipline, bad food, and low pay—glory be damned. Life on a merchantman was easier and more rewarding, and Suckling had to use considerable persuasion to coax fourteen-year-old Horatio back into the service. In the end, however, the boy relented, taking command of the longboat of Suckling's guardship stationed at the Nore, the great sandbank at the mouth of the Thames.

It was dull duty, but before long Horatio captured a chance for genuine adventure, winning permission to join a two-ship expedition searching for an Arctic route to India. The vessels sailed from Spitsbergen early in June of 1773, but they were little more than two months out of port when great monoliths of ice closed in on all sides, forcing them to turn back. Though a failure, the expedition afforded evidence that Nelson's childhood fearlessness had not only persisted into adolescence but threatened to spill over into recklessness. Bent on securing a polar bear skin for his father, he stole off his ship and onto the ice one night, found a bear, and when his musket misfired, was about to try to brain it with his gun butt when a blank shot from the ship scared the animal away. His courage, so abundant, needed tempering and direction.

When he was fifteen, Nelson secured a berth on the frigate *Seahorse* for a long voyage to exotic ports in India and Ceylon and across the Arabian Sea and Persian Gulf. But in the East he was felled by malaria, becoming so ill that he had to be transferred to another ship, the *Dolphin*, bound for England.

Exhausted and emaciated, drifting in and out of delirium, he became suicidally depressed. But as the *Dolphin* forged northward, he had a feverish vision that altered his life forever. A "radiant orb" beckoned to him, he later wrote, and "a sudden glow of patriotism was kindled within me, and presented my King and Country as my Patron. 'Well, then,' I exclaimed, 'I will be a hero and, confiding in Providence, I will brave every danger.'"

Horatio Nelson had by now grown into a thin young man of no more than average height, prone to melancholy, of indifferent looks and uncertain health. But from the day of his epiphany onward—years before every Englishman would know him as "The Hero"—he would seldom doubt his destiny.

As the young Bonaparte would come to see his fate as conquest and empire, so the young Nelson embraced a vision of his own, more modest star, a providential future of service, honor, and glory.

*   *   *

For a time it seemed that Nelson was sailing toward that destiny before the wind, rising in the navy's ranks with uncommon speed—due partly, perhaps, to his uncle's influence, but mostly to his own initiative and talent. By regulation, lieutenants were supposed to

MANPOWER FOR SEA POWER

Life at sea may not have been a particularly attractive prospect for a man in Georgian England, but it was always an option: the Royal Navy was constantly, chronically, in need of sailors. Its peacetime strength in 1792 was fifteen thousand men, but in five years it increased eightfold, and by 1813 the number stood at one hundred and fifty thousand—this in a nation whose population was only about 10 million. England's navy may have been the envy of the world, but it was not at all uncommon for her warships to sail undermanned.

France drafted her seamen, but mass conscription in England in Horatio Nelson's day was unthinkable, so protective were Britons of the individual liberties they had acquired over the centuries. The British government therefore had to rely on a rather arbitrary system of blandishments coupled with coercion.

Captains were responsible for manning their own ships, and a famous commander such as Nelson found it comparatively easy to assemble a crew. Captains commonly put up posters advertising available berths. Some of these offered prospects of glory, but more usually they appealed to greed, with promises (most of them wildly inflated) of prize money. The government also offered modest bonuses for seamen who enlisted.

If all else failed, there were the press-gangs, groups of six or seven sailors, supervised by a junior officer, who roamed the streets bent on recruitment. Impressment, a practice that dated back to feudal times, was popularly viewed as an infringement on personal freedom, and press-gangs were often satirized as brutes who dragged off hapless civilians by force to serve on His Majesty's ships, whether they craved that honor or not. In fact, however, most gangs followed the rule that only professional seamen could be impressed (although the term might be broadly interpreted), and force was used only as a last resort. More often they merely hung recruitment posters or tried to talk their quarry into joining up.

Early in his career Nelson was assigned to oversee a press-gang, although he, like most captains, deplored impressment on practical as well as ethical grounds; a pressed sailor was not apt to be as useful as a willing volunteer, nor as good for morale. Nevertheless, most officers accepted the practice as a necessary evil for keeping the fleet at sea.

A typical anti-impressment cartoon shows a spindly landlubber being cudgeled into naval service. Brutal or not, impressment never supplied more than a fraction of the navy's manpower—about one-third at the height of the war against Napoleon.

be at least twenty, but Nelson was only eighteen when, after the requisite interview with the Admiralty, he was promoted in April 1777. Some seventeen months later he was elevated to first lieutenant, and three months after that to commander. Six months later he was a full captain, commanding a frigate. It took skill—and perhaps connections—to rise to captain, but promotion after that, to rear admiral and beyond, came on the basis of seniority alone. Young as he was, it seemed all but inevitable that in due course he would attain flag rank.

But while time and patience could create admirals, heroes were forged only in battle, and Nelson fought none at sea. England was by now at war on several fronts: with the frac-

A watercolor portrait of Captain Horatio Nelson (above), painted by his friend Captain Cuthbert Collingwood in 1784, shows Nelson wearing a wig to conceal temporary baldness, the result of a bout with yellow fever. Fanny Nelson (right) was fretful and inefficient in practical matters, which irritated her husband, but their correspondence suggests the Nelsons were an affectionate couple in the early years.

tious American colonies, with France for helping the American rebels, and with France's ally, Spain. The New World was the war's crucial arena, as the European combatants tried variously to assault their enemies' colonies or defend their own and to disrupt each other's transAtlantic commercial and military shipping. Despite the plenitude of adversaries, however, Captain Nelson—though he saw duty in the West Indies, Central America, and Canada—was often relegated to escorting convoys.

Ashore, however, he did acquire a wife. On the West Indian island of Nevis, he wooed and won a genteel widow named Frances Nisbet, the niece of John Richardson Herbert, president of the island's governing council. Fanny, as she was called, had been born on Nevis, the daughter of a judge. Her mother had died when the girl was young, and after her father's death, she married Josiah Nisbet, the physician who had attended him in his final illness. The couple moved to England, but a year and a half later Nisbet died there, leaving Fanny with an infant son. She and the boy returned to Nevis, where she moved in with her uncle, a widower, to help him oversee his large and elegant household.

When Nelson paid a call on that household one morning, President Herbert found the young captain, who adored children, roughhousing under the dining room table with Fanny's five-year-old son. The captain and the widow met a few days later at dinner, and Fanny thanked him for the "great partiality" he had shown to her little boy.

Thus began a decorous courtship that lasted six months before Nelson proposed. Fanny accepted, although with her fiancé away at sea much of the time, the marriage would not take place for another eighteen months. Nelson wrote to his Uncle Maurice about Fanny, saying that "her mental accomplishments are superior to most persons of either sex" and that "my affection for her is fixed upon that solid basis of esteem and regard that I trust can only increase by a longer knowledge of her."

If practical, such sentiments were hardly passionate, but Nelson may have felt that he had outgrown passion. In his younger days his mad infatuations with two other young ladies had come to nothing, and now, in his late twenties, he may have thought that suitability, and companionship to ease a sea captain's loneliness, had their own allure. Fanny, if no beauty, was pleasant looking, fashionable in dress, and a competent hostess. She played the piano well and spoke French. A few months older than he, she had a placid dignity, a quiet charm that was in no way flighty. They married on Nevis in 1787, and he thought himself a lucky man.

Wedded bliss aside, however, Nelson was entering one of the most frustrating periods of his life. After England lost its American colonies in 1781, hostilities with France abated, and the navy once again began decommissioning ships. Nelson's frigate was paid off in 1787, and the captain found himself beached, on half pay, the usual fate of officers without a ship. He and his wife and stepson settled into uneventful domesticity with his father at Burnham Thorpe, and Nelson tried to

involve his mind in family matters and local pursuits. But, in fact, he had only one abiding interest: getting back to sea. For more than five years he vainly petitioned the Admiralty for a ship, his dreams of heroism unraveling with every passing week and month. He was nearing his mid-thirties now, and it appeared that greatness might elude him after all.

But again history intervened. In January of 1793 the French revolutionaries beheaded their king and queen and seemed bent on exporting their blood-soaked republicanism. Royalist England prepared to resist and offered a haven for French aristocrats fleeing the guillotine. On January 30 an exultant Nelson received a commission to command his first ship of the line, the 64-gun *Agamemnon*. Two days later France declared war on England.

* * *

The *Agamemnon* was not among England's biggest warships, but during action in the Americas she had proved herself one of the fastest, and even after his years on her were over, she would remain Nelson's favorite ship. "I have the pleasure in telling you that my ship is without exception the finest 64 in the service," he wrote to Fanny soon after going on board. "*Agamemnon* sails admirably. We think her better than any ship in the fleet."

She was also well manned. Anxious to minimize the number of resentful, press-ganged seaman in his crew, Nelson had advertised for volunteers not only in London but also in Norfolk and neighboring Suffolk, where he was already known. Thus he sailed with a high

THE SHIPS: HOW THEY RATED

The British Navy assigned each of its warships to one of six categories, or rates, depending not on the ship's quality but solely on the number of cannons she carried and the bulk required to accommodate them. Thus, a first-rate might be in no way superior to a third-rate in speed or sturdiness or maneuverability or even fame, but only in size and armament. Each type had its peculiar virtues and flaws, and all contributed to England's preeminence at sea. But only vessels of the first three rates, those carrying 60 guns or more, were accounted ships of the line or sail of the line— ships big and powerful enough to take their place on the British battle line in major sea engagements.

FIRST-RATES

These three-deckers, the flagships of the fleet, bore from 100 to 112 cannons each. A first-rate might be as long as 206 feet on the lower gun deck and carry a crew of 875 men— more if an admiral and his entourage were aboard. The *Victory* was the most famous of this category. Because of their bulk, first-rates tended to be slower than their smaller sisters, but they were the most powerful English arsenals afloat. They were also the most expensive, costing about £100,000 each ($105,000,000 at current rates), so the navy had fewer than a dozen in service at any one time.

Bristling with cannons, a first-rate British ship of the line takes on stores in this painting by J. M. W. Turner. The Victory, Nelson's three-deck flagship at the Battle of Trafalgar, looked much like this.

SECOND-RATES

A second-rate carried from 90 to 98 cannons on her three gun decks, along with 743 men. She was 195 feet long—only a little smaller than a first-rate, which she resembled in nearly every respect.

THIRD-RATES

The most varied ship-of-the-line category, the third-rates included ships bearing 64, 74, or 80 guns. An 80-gun ship had three decks; a 74 or 64 had two. Commensurate crew sizes were 724, 620, or 494 men. There were more 74s in the British navy than any other kind of ship, since they had time and again proved to offer the best balance of speed and power. The *Vanguard*, Nelson's flagship at the Nile, was a 74.

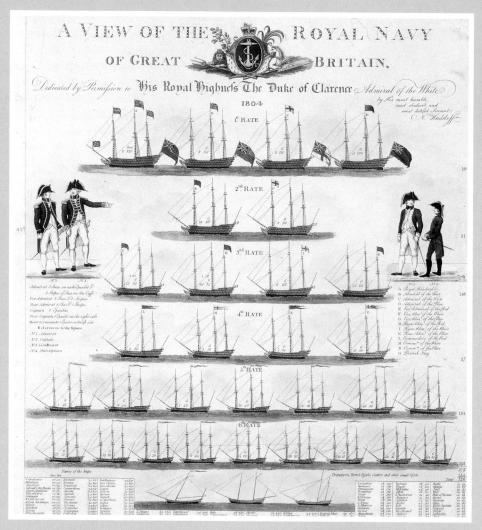

FOURTH-RATES

A fourth-rate was a two-decker that mounted from 50 to 56 guns and carried 345 men. She could be built for only about £26,000 ($27,000,000), was inexpensive to maintain, and functioned well at the head of cruiser squadrons, but by Nelson's day there were only a few fourth-rates in service; they were too undersized and lightly armed for the battle line, and they were not as fast as frigates. The 50-gun *Leander*, part of Nelson's squadron at the Battle of the Nile, was a fourth-rate.

FIFTH-RATES

These were the frigates, the swift raiders, scouts, and watchdogs of the fleet. They were single-deckers and ranged in length from 130 to 150 feet. Frigates carried 32, 36, 38, or 44 guns, and crews numbered from 217 to 297 men, most of them enthusiastic volunteers. Frigates were the ships of choice for bringing down enemy merchantmen. Captured merchant ships and their cargoes, as well as captured warships, were put before an Admiralty court that usually decreed their sale. Proceeds were

divided among the officers and crew. A captain got three-eighths, of which one-eighth went to the commander of his fleet or station; officers shared two-eighths; midshipmen and warrant officers, one; and the rest of the crew divided the remaining two-eighths.

SIXTH-RATES

Sixth-rates were small frigates, agile 125-foot ships that carried 20, 24, or 28 guns and crews of 138, 158, and 198. These vessels were useful as couriers and convoy escorts and were cheap to build, each one costing about £10,000 ($11,000,000).

percentage of willing seamen, and it was among them that he perfected his style of inspirational leadership, his singular oneness of feeling and purpose with his officers and men.

To no small degree, Nelson got respect because he gave it. He was a strict disciplinarian, as quick as the next captain to order a flogging if he felt one was in order. But he was neither unfair nor unapproachable, and he fully understood that his sailors, even the lowest born and least schooled among them, were capable of remarkable loyalty and courage. He therefore did all he could to see that they were promptly paid and as well fed and well clothed as possible and that their living quarters were decently ventilated and comparatively free of vermin. And—ever his father's son—he arranged for every man to have a Bible, whether he could read it or not.

Beyond such homely necessities, however, the *Agamemnon*'s captain gave his men a gift of incalculable value: pride in who they were and what they did. If he demanded the best of them (and he did; no captain drilled his gunners and other seamen longer or harder), he lavished praise when they delivered. He was quick to shoulder blame and share glory, and for this his men rewarded him with loyalty and affection. Even in a generation of superb officers, few captains were as esteemed by their crews as he.

With his own officers Nelson tended to be collegial, seeking their counsel from time to time and including them in some decision making. It was a style that ran against tradition, for British captains, whose power aboard their own ships was virtually absolute, were usu-

ally autocrats, neither inviting nor welcoming opinions from underlings. Nelson's trust had the practical effect of making his lieutenants more confident, self-reliant, and resourceful—and unswervingly committed to their leader.

"Captain Nelson is acknowledged to be one of the finest characters in the service," young midshipman William Hoste of the *Agamemnon* summed up in a letter to his father, "and is universally beloved by his men and officers."

The ship's first mission under Nelson took her to the Mediterranean. Preparing for war, the Royal Navy had divided itself into two fleets. One patrolled the Atlantic and home waters, while the other, under Samuel, Lord Hood, was charged with protecting Britain's Mediterranean interests and sealing up France's southern ports. The *Agamemnon* was assigned to Hood, and by mid-July she was one of fifteen men-of-war blockading Toulon.

When the city turned royalist at the end of August and Hood prepared to defend it against a Jacobin counterattack, he dispatched Nelson to seek reinforcements from England's Italian ally, the Kingdom of Naples. The mission was a success: King Ferdinand promised six thousand troops for Toulon's defense. The king, whose domain included Sicily and most of southern Italy, even deigned to dine aboard the *Agamemnon*—an honor that only a royalist as ardent as Nelson could have relished, since Ferdinand was a thoroughgoing lout. A scion of the Spanish Bourbons, he had been reared by parents who, believing that education might exacerbate the insanity that ran rampant in the family, spared him much contact with it. As a result, his only real interests were hunting and philandering.

More cultivated company was to be had in Naples, however, in the person of Sir William Hamilton, the highly respected British ambassador, who was also an accomplished antiquarian and vulcanologist. Nelson and Hamilton took an immediate liking to each other, and the captain spent his four-day stopover in Naples as a guest of the sixty-three-year-old diplomat—and of his ravishing twenty-eight-year-old wife, Emma, a lady of humble origins and a rather shady past.

Nothing suggests that Emma Hamilton immediately became the grand passion of Nelson's life, but he was sufficiently impressed to write to Fanny that Lady Hamilton was "a young woman of amiable manners, and who does honour to the station to which she is raised." Fanny would, to her sorrow, hear much more about Emma in years to come.

About a month after leaving Naples, Nelson finally got his first taste of sea battle. In late October, the *Agamemnon* was sailing off the Sardinian coast when her lookout spotted on the far horizon a squadron of four French frigates. Piling on sail, Nelson's ship gave chase, finally overtaking the rearmost of the frigates, the *Melpomène*. Approaching on a perpendicular course, Nelson was able to use only his bow guns, while the frigate let loose broadsides against the bigger ship. In a four-hour fight the *Melpomène* was badly damaged, and Nelson would probably have captured or sunk her had not the other three frigates come to her aid. By that time, in any case, the *Agamemnon* was also mauled, her foreyard and two of her masts damaged. After confer-

ring with his lieutenants as to whether the ship was "fit to go into action with such a superior force against us, without some small refit and refreshment for our people," the captain decided to break off the engagement and seek a friendly port for repairs.

His first sea skirmish had been a qualified success, if not exactly the heroic display to which he aspired. Oddly, the making of Nelson the Hero would begin not at sea but on land.

*   *   *

After the fall of Toulon—the French victory engineered by a brash young artillery officer named Napoleon Bonaparte, who was just beginning his rise—Admiral Hood turned his attention to Bonaparte's native island of Corsica, which was in revolt against its French occupiers. Ousting the French would give the British a valuable base for her Mediterranean operations.

With the *Agamemnon* repaired and now at the head of a squadron of frigates, Nelson joined Hood at Corsica in January 1794 and began raiding forts and ships along the coast. Hood took the town of San Fiorenzo in early February and with this toehold set his sights on the heavily fortified coastal town of Bastia. The admiral wanted a joint attack by land and sea, but to his consternation and Nelson's, the army refused to support him. So he decided to attack on his own, using sailors and the 1,248 marines—seagoing soldiers assigned to ships of the line—who were under his authority. For artillery he would simply move some of the *Agamemnon's*

THE GUNS: THUNDER AT SEA

The world's best navy may not have had the world's best ships. Some experts believe the French men-of-war of the late eighteenth century were faster and better proportioned, and even Nelson conceded that the Spanish built "very fine ships"—and very big ones. But whatever its virtues or nationality, a ship of the line was first, last, and always a floating platform for artillery, and when it came to gunnery and gunners, the English were in class by themselves.

CANNONS

Cannons of the Royal Navy were named for the weight of the shot they fired: 32-pounders (the standard big gun in first-rate ships), 24-pounders, 18-pounders, and 12-, 9-, and 6-pounders. There were also carronades, stubby guns that, while not part of a ship's official gun count, were usually on board, especially at the bow and stern. Only a yard long, carronades could nevertheless fire several weights of shot—the heaviest an incredible 68 pounds—and were devastating at close range.

Made of cast iron and mounted on wheeled wooden carriages, all cannons were tremendously heavy. A 9-foot-long 18-pounder, for example—a medium-sized gun—weighed 2,388 pounds. When idle, the weapons were "housed," kept tightly lashed to the ship's side to prevent movement: a 2-ton loose cannon on a rolling deck could kill men and even hole a 2-foot-thick oak hull. The lashings were cast loose for action, allowing the guns to move back and forth along runners. These helped absorb the weapons'

The muscular labors of a British navy gun crew in the midst of battle are portrayed in this contemporary painting by Thomas Stothard.

mighty recoil and let them be run out of the gun port for firing and back in for reloading. Recoil was further braked with breeching, heavy rope attached to a knob at the back of the gun and anchored on both sides to iron rings in the ship's side.

The cannons, all muzzle loaded, fired a variety of projectiles, the most common being the iron cannonball. A 32-pound ball could knock a hole in an enemy hull at a distance of half a mile. Usually, however, the distances were not that great. Gunners commanded by a captain like Nelson, who liked to slug it out yardarm-to-

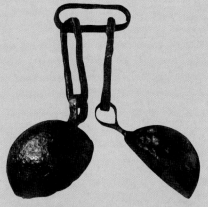

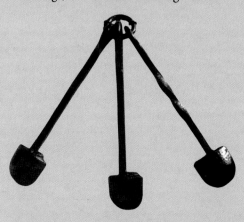

yardarm with his foes, could send a ball into one side of a ship and out the other, its passage marked by flying dagger-sized oak splinters that cost many a seaman an arm, a leg, or his life. Grapeshot (small iron balls held together in a canvas bag that exploded on firing) and similar canister shot were antipersonnel weapons, while chain shot (iron balls or half balls joined together with a chain link) or bar shot (an assemblage of bars, tipped with a half ball at one end and joined together at the other with a single link) could shred sails and slice through the stoutest rigging. A cannon might be loaded with one shot at a time or with two or even three.

Whatever the shot, the propellant was gunpowder. A first-rate might carry 35 tons of it in the powder magazine situated deep in her hold, as safe from fire as possible. Fire in the magazine usually spelled death for a ship and most of her hands.

GUN CREWS

Guns were manned by crews who worked both the starboard and larboard sides of the ship. A big gun like a 32-pounder required a crew of up to fifteen men; the smaller guns, fewer. For any cannon the crew

included the captain of the gun, a sponger, and powder monkeys, as well as seamen whose noncombat duties extended beyond the guns, such as firemen, boarders, and sail trimmers. Sometimes marines lent muscle to haul the cumbersome cannons back and forth. These men drilled together so constantly that they required few words, performing their destructive ballet almost by instinct.

Preparing a gun for action, they first opened its port, cast loose its lashings, and removed a bung called

the tompion that kept its muzzle watertight. Then they hooked on three tackles—one on each side of the gun for running it out and the third, the train tackle, behind for hauling it back—and affixed the breeching to its knob. When the cannon had been run in and was held steady by men holding the breeching and train tackle, a young powder monkey handed the sponger a cartridge, a flannel bag holding six pounds of gunpowder. The sponger rammed the cartridge into the breech. He knew it was in place when the gun captain, feeling for it with a priming iron inserted into the touchhole (the vent

through which the gunpowder would be ignited), shouted, "Home!" Then the shot was rammed in, followed by a wad to hold it in place.

The gun was now loaded, and its crew hauled it forward by its side tackles until the muzzle stuck out through the gun port as far as it would go. The captain ruptured the cartridge with his priming iron and inserted into the touchhole a quill filled with fine gunpowder.

Aiming was primitive, perhaps because in battles fought at point-bank range, aim was not particularly important. The cannon's muzzle could be turned slightly to the left or right by shoving at the gun carriage with crowbars or trimming it with handspikes. The muzzle could also be elevated a bit with handspikes or lowered by wedging a piece of wood called a quoin under the breech. These niceties were far less important, however, than the roll of the ship. Accuracy depended mainly on calculating the time when a deck's rise or fall would best bring the gun to bear on the enemy.

When the time was right, the gun captain used a flintlock to ignite the powder in the quill, which in turn

Along with cannon balls, missiles fired by naval guns included, from top to bottom, chain shot, bar shot, and elongating shot. All expanded in flight, the better to mangle sails, spars, and rigging.

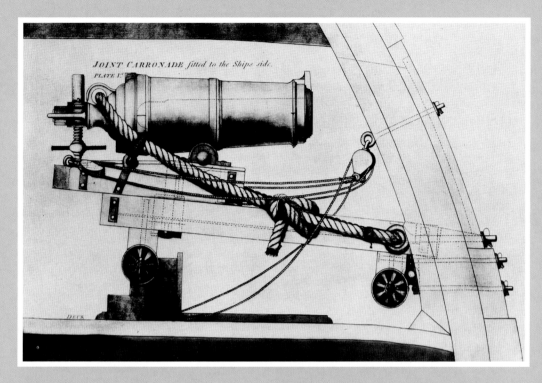

Short but vicious, the carronade was called "the smasher" by the British. It was devastating at close range because it could fire even heavier loads than the long-barreled cannons— up to 64 pounds. Another advantage of the little gun was that it required less space to mount and operate. Carronades were added to England's naval arsenal in 1779, and they were so effective that the French called them "devil guns."

touched off the powder in the breech. There was a thunderous roar and a bloom of noxious black smoke, and shot screamed out of the muzzle at 1,200 feet per second. Recoil sent the gun flying back against the breech and bouncing forward again, to be steadied by strong hands on the train tackle. When it was still, the muzzle was cleaned with a corkscrew-like device called a worm and again with a wet mop wielded by the sponger to extinguish any stray sparks.

The whole maneuver was at once precise and backbreaking, but the well-trained British gun crews could get off three rounds in little more than two minutes—speed that meant victory in the great sea battles of the time.

This 32-pound cannon was the largest long-barreled gun in standard use in Nelson's navy. The replica shown here is on the restored Victory, anchored at Portsmouth.

cannons on shore. On the night of April 3, the troops were disembarked just north of Bastia, and by noon the next day eight of the ship's cannons, along with eight mortars sent from Naples, had come ashore. Under Nelson's direction, crewmen anchored the big guns to sledges and with Herculean effort began dragging them up the rocky mountainside below the town. Eight days after the landing, the English began bombardment.

With the French putting up a valiant defense, the siege went on and on. "We are in high spirits," Nelson wrote to his wife. "I am very busy, yet own I am in all my glory." On May 21, after holding out for thirty-seven days, Bastia fell.

Nelson was ecstatic at the victory—at least until he read Hood's published dispatches on it, which failed to give him the credit he thought he deserved. "The whole operation of the siege was carried on through Lord Hood's letters to me," he wrote to Fanny. "I was the mover of it—I was the cause of its success." The remarks, while possibly justified, were typically peevish and self-congratulatory. Of the tragic flaws allotted to great men, Nelson's was vanity. He craved glory and recognition, and when he did not get them, he could be petulant and petty.

But his anger at Hood, whom he once called "certainly the best officer I ever saw," soon cooled, and when the admiral decided to go after another French stronghold on Corsica, the town of Calvi, Nelson again commanded the onshore assault. Calvi fell on August 12 after another grueling siege, this one costlier than Bastia. Casualties on both sides were high, and of the two thou-

sand English survivors, half came down with malaria and other ailments. Nelson himself was ill again. Worse, Calvi cost him an eye. On July 12 a cannonball hitting a parapet he was standing beside flung up a storm of debris into his face and chest. A splinter hit his right eye, blinding him.

To add to his troubles, the captain was losing a commander in chief whom, on the whole, he greatly admired. Hood was returning to England, to be replaced by Vice Admiral Sir William Hotham. The aggressive, combative Hood, a man after Nelson's own heart, had been something of an anomaly among the older generation of British admirals. Hotham was more typical of the breed—a conservative, by-the-book admiral, content with marginal victories, lacking the killer instinct that urged total destruction of the enemy. And in the first encounter of his Mediterranean command, Hotham ran true to form.

On the morning of March 11, 1795, the admiral and his fleet of fifteen warships overtook a French line of the same number headed for Corsica under Admiral Pierre Martin. The fast *Agamemnon* was at the head of the British column. As Nelson approached the enemy ships, the 84-gun *Ça Ira*, third from the rear of the French line, ran into the vessel ahead of her and lost her fore and main topmasts. Crippled, she dropped astern of the line, and Nelson moved in for the kill. Avoiding exposure to the bigger ship's broadsides, the *Agamemnon* tacked back and forth astern of her for two and a half hours, pulling close and then coming about so the well-trained English gunners could decimate her with broadsides of their own. By the afternoon Nelson wrote, "The

Samuel, Viscount Hood, the outspoken and aggressive admiral shown here in a portrait by James Northcote, was remembered by Horatio Nelson as "the greatest sea officer I ever knew."

Ça Ira was a perfect wreck, her sails hanging in tatters, mizzen, topmast, mizzen topsail and cross-jack yards shot away." About a hundred of her crewmen were dead, while the *Agamemnon* had suffered only seven wounded.

By now Admiral Martin was turning his line to help the stricken ship, and it looked as though a major battle was in the making when Hotham, fearing the *Agamemnon* might be cut off and surrounded, hoisted the signal to break off action. By the next morning the *Ça Ira* was under tow by a frigate, and the British took both the frigate and the wounded man-of-war. But to Nelson's unutterable scorn, Hotham declined to order pursuit of the rest of the escaping French fleet. Throwing decorum to the wind, Nelson went aboard Hotham's flagship and begged the admiral to give chase and make the French fight, gambling for a victory such as "the Annals of England never produced." But Hotham was no gambler. Corsica had been defended and two ships taken, and that was enough,

"We have done very well," he blandly assured his livid captain.

"My disposition cannot bear tame and slow measures," Nelson raged in a subsequent letter to Fanny. "I wish to be an Admiral and in command of the English fleet; I should very soon either do much or be ruined."

His contempt for his chief was made complete when, in July, the British had another chance at the French fleet, this time at Hyères off France's Côte d'Azur. After a single skirmish in which the *Agamemnon*

The formidable John Jervis, earl of St. Vincent, admiral of the fleet, and from 1801 to 1805 first lord of the Admiralty, admired Nelson's daring and fostered his career, but he later came to deplore his subordinate's private life.

and three sister ships blew a French man-of-war out of the water, the timid Hotham once again signaled to withdraw.

"Thus ended our second meeting with these gentry," an enraged Nelson wrote. "In the forenoon we had every prospect of taking every Ship in the Fleet, and at noon it was almost certain we should have the six rear ships."

Had Hotham been less cautious or Nelson been in command, the early years of the Napoleonic wars might have gone quite differently. As it was, however, the sea war was indecisive, while on land Napoleon pushed the Austrians out of Italy and closed northern Italian ports to British ships. By the fall of 1796, England would once again stand virtually alone against France, Spain, and Holland, and by year's end, the British would have lost hard-won Corsica and given up all of England's Mediterranean holdings except Gibraltar.

* * *

Frustrated and weary, Nelson thought late in 1795—not for the first time—about retiring to England. The war was going Bonaparte's way, and there seemed little that a half-blind, outranked British naval officer could do about it. His beloved *Agamemnon*, aging and battle scarred herself, would soon wallow off to home shores for a much-needed overhaul, and her captain was feeling at low ebb.

Then came news that revived his hopes of glory: Hotham had been recalled to England, to be replaced in the Mediterranean by Sir John Jervis. Like Hood—and, of course, like Nelson himself—Jervis was a man of action, a fighter, and a superb strategist and leader. At age sixty-three he was, in fact, the most respected admiral in the British fleet. "Reports say the French will have their fleet at sea again," Nelson wrote to Fanny after Jervis's appointment. "If they do I think they will now lose the whole of them, for we have a man of business at our head."

From their first meeting, in January of 1796 aboard Jervis's flagship *Victory*, the admiral and his like-minded subordinate shared a special affinity, Jervis treating Nelson "more as an associate than a subordinate," the captain wrote. It was a sign of Jervis's trust and approval that in March he appointed Nelson to the temporary rank of commodore. His broad pendant flying on the 74-gun *Captain*, Nelson would now command a squadron of two ships of the line and four frigates.

While the appointment was gratifying, the commodore's earliest duties under Jervis were both sad and inglorious. England was pulling out of the Mediterranean, and her ships there were assigned to help evacuate British personnel and to try to prevent seaborne supplies from reaching France's victorious land armies. Nelson carried out these tasks "in sackcloth and ashes," he wrote, certain that London was underestimating the worth of her own navy, "whose fleets are equal to meet the World in arms." But even as the Mediterranean fleet sailed north into the Atlantic, he was afforded the chance to prove his point and to approach at last the threshold of his long-sought destiny.

On St. Valentine's Day 1797, Jervis's fleet of fifteen battleships encountered a Spanish fleet off the Portuguese Cape of St. Vincent, making for Cádiz. Aboard

the flagship *Victory*, Robert Calder, captain of the fleet, relayed the reports of scouting vessels to his admiral:

"There are eight sail of the line, Sir John."

"Very well, sir."

"There are twenty sail of the line, Sir John."

"Very well, sir."

"There are twenty-five sail of the line . . . twenty-seven, Sir John. Near twice our own . . ."

"Enough sir!" Jervis shouted. "The die is cast, and if there were fifty sail I will go through them."

The Spaniards were in a ragged formation—two groups of ships with a large gap between. Jervis's ships were in a tight, disciplined line, which he now aimed like an arrow between the two groups, dividing them from each other. Leading the way on the *Culloden* was the fiery Thomas Troubridge, Nelson's friend since the two had been midshipmen on the *Seahorse* years earlier. Bringing up the rear was the *Excellent*, commanded by another old friend, Cuthbert Collingwood, whom Nelson had first met in the West Indies.

Having separated the two Spanish groups and driven the smaller one out of the battle with thunderous broadsides, Jervis now abandoned his tight line of battle and divided his force into three groups. He turned them northward, intending to envelop the larger body of Spanish ships with his entire force and bring about a decisive battle. But even as the signals flew from the *Victory* ordering this complex

Nelson achieves glory in a stunning display of bravery at the Battle of Cape St. Vincent. In a furious rush, he and his fellow boarders leap from H.M.S. Captain *(left) on to the decks of the third-rated Spanish ship,* San Nicolás. *The first-rated ship,* San José, *is on the right.*

maneuver, Nelson, lying fourth from the rear of the British line, noticed that the Spanish were trying to escape by running across the sterns of the rearmost British ships. To stop them, he turned the *Captain* out of the formation and headed straight for the retreating enemy. Faced with such a determined onslaught, the Spanish swerved back onto their original course. But their hesitation had given the rest of the British fleet time to catch up, and within moments the Spanish were being battered on all sides by murderous British broadsides.

In her headlong rush, the *Captain* had been exposed to the broadsides of at least seven Spanish ships, including the 130-gun behemoth *Santissima Trinidad*, one of the largest men-of-war in the world. Her sails and rigging were in shreds, her foretopmast shattered, and her wheel smashed. By any reasonable standard, she and her crew had more than done their duty.

But Nelson's moment of greatest glory was still to come. Two Spanish ships collided with each other while reeling away from the fierce fire from Collingwood's *Excellent*. Nelson ordered the *Captain* to be laid alongside the nearest, the 80-gun *San Nicolás*, and as the two ships crashed together, he shouted for a boarding party. Then, with sword drawn, he led his men in a headlong leap onto the stern of the Spanish ship. Sailors and marines surged after him, some vaulting from bulwark to bulwark, others, cutlasses clenched in their teeth, running along the bowsprit and hurling themselves onto the *San Nicolás*'s rigging.

Under fire and choking on the heavy, acrid smoke from the hot cannons, Nelson and his men fought their way to the quarterdeck—there to find the Spanish ensign already being hauled down by Edward Berry, one of Nelson's officers. Even as the guns below them pounded at the British adversaries, several Spanish officers on the quarterdeck offered Nelson their swords in surrender.

By now the *San Nicolás* was on fire, and on the side opposite her collision point with the *Captain*, her rigging had become snarled with that of her sister ship, the three-decker 114-gun *San José*. From aloft on the taller ship, a burst of musket fire rained down on the *San Nicolás*'s quarterdeck as her officers were surrendering. About twenty Spaniards were wounded and seven of Nelson's men killed. Enraged, Nelson determined to use the *San Nicolás* as a bridge to take the *San José* as well. After calling up reinforcements from the *Captain*, he led the charge himself, flinging himself onto the big first-rate. The *San José* surrendered shortly thereafter.

In a feat that became popularly known as "Nelson's Patent Bridge for Boarding First-Rates," a white-clad Horatio Nelson and his men storm across the captured Spanish ship San Nicolás *to take possession of her sister ship, the* San José, *at the Battle of Cape St. Vincent. Artist George Jones sanitized the scene. At this point in the battle, Nelson's uniform was actually in tatters and his face blackened by smoke.*

As victories go, the Battle of Cape St. Vincent was as glorious as even Nelson could have hoped. Facing a force almost twice its size, the British fleet had won the day and taken two more Spanish ships in addition to the two Nelson had captured personally.

There was one bothersome technicality; in pulling the *Captain* out of the English battle line on his own initiative, Nelson had violated the long-standing navy rule forbidding any ship to break formation. But he was hardly the first officer to do so; the rule had worn threadbare long before. Besides, he believed he was acting in accordance with Jervis's overall plan and that Jervis would back him up. He was quite right, as he learned when he presented himself aboard the *Victory* after the battle.

"The Admiral received me on the quarterdeck," Nelson wrote, "and having embraced me, said he could not sufficiently thank me and used every kind expression which could not fail to make me happy."

Jervis certainly had every reason for gratitude; in the wake of the battle, he was made earl of St. Vincent. Nelson himself was given a knighthood, the coveted Order of the Bath, and the victory was made even sweeter when he learned that he had won it not as a captain but as a rear admiral. The news of his promotion had failed to reach him beforehand.

* * *

Nelson's career seemed to follow a pattern of peaks and troughs, the lows seldom of his own making. Cape St. Vincent had been his highest peak thus far, a triumph that made him famous and won him the love and acclaim he so craved from his victory-starved countrymen. "Joy sparkles in every eye," his proud father wrote to him, "and desponding Britain draws back her sable veil, and smiles." But St. Vincent would be followed hard upon by the first failure of a major operation under Nelson's command, the disaster at Santa Cruz de Tenerife in the Canary Islands.

Since April, Earl St. Vincent and Nelson had been discussing an amphibious operation against the Spanish-held islands. The army, however, saw little point in the venture, regarding it (correctly) as primarily a raid intended to afford the navy's officers and crew lavish prize money in the event that a Spanish treasure ship happened to be in port at Tenerife. In no way dismayed, Nelson was sure he could manage without army support. After all, he had succeeded on Corsica with only sailors and marines; he would succeed on Tenerife as well. The prospect shifted from tempting to irresistible when it was learned that a large treasure ship, *El Principe d'Asturias*, had arrived in Santa Cruz from Manila. Personal rewards aside, taking such a ship would deprive Spain of much-needed wealth.

In July, St. Vincent outfitted his junior admiral with a squadron of a cutter, three frigates, the 50-gun *Leander*, and three 74s commanded by Nelson's handpicked captains: Ralph Miller on Nelson's flagship, the *Theseus*; Thomas Troubridge on the *Culloden*; and on the *Zealous*, Samuel Hood, cousin of Admiral Samuel Hood, who had been Nelson's commander at Corsica. Nelson's orders were to capture the port of Santa Cruz, destroy any enemy warships, and capture *El Principe d'Asturias*.

Santa Cruz, on Tenerife's east coast on a plain enclosed by steep outcroppings of volcanic rock, lay behind a series of small forts strung along the shore, their cannons protecting both the town and the harbor. The harbor itself, open except for a breakwater, offered safe anchorage only close to shore, under the guns. Nelson's plan for taking the town, perfected in consultation with his officers, depended heavily on the element of surprise.

next morning the warships would appear in the harbor, ready to bombard the town or accept surrender. There might be resistance, of course, but Nelson was inclined to equate Spanish soldiers with Spanish sailors, who had never impressed him.

The operation began on July 20, and from the beginning, everything went wrong. Nelson had counted on the northeast trade winds to sweep his ships close to shore, but instead the winds blew capriciously from land, and the current ran against his ships as well. Troubridge declined to land his men under such conditions until he could consult with Nelson. Thus, when the three 74s appeared in the harbor the next morning, they found their quarry not subdued but thoroughly alarmed by the sight of the enemy squadron in its harbor.

Weather kept the British at bay for two more days, giving the Spanish, who outnumbered their invaders, time to man every parapet and prepare every gun. Even though the element of surprise was now utterly gone, Nelson persisted. On July 24 he implemented a plan to try to land his men on the breakwater. Leading them, he would fight his way to Santa Cruz's town square.

As night fell, about seven hundred men made their way onto boats that rolled beside the ships in heavy seas,

Thomas Rowlandson's famous series of aquatints depicting England's shipboard personnel include this one of a captain of the marines. These seagoing soldiers were especially useful in boardings and shore actions.

After dark his frigates would land men under Troubridge's command while the three big warships stayed out of sight, well offshore. Troubridge's party of about one thousand seamen and marines would take the two forts that protected the town on the east. The

His arm shattered by musket fire in the abortive 1797 raid on Tenerife, Nelson collapses into the arms of a young lieutenant, his stepson, Josiah Nisbet. Nisbet probably saved the admiral's life by getting him back to the Theseus *for treatment. Over time, however, Nisbet proved a disappointing officer, and he abandoned his naval career to become a succesful businessman.*

concealed from Spanish lookouts for a time by the swells and by darkness and rain. The cutter *Fox* carried another eighty sailors and marines, and a newly captured Spanish merchantman, another one hundred and eighty. But as the boats neared the shore, the sky suddenly glared with rockets and with the flash of firing cannons and muskets. The Spanish had spotted them. Bullets and grapeshot spurted down from the forts and belched from the heavily defended breakwater. The *Fox* was struck and sank, going down with her captain and most of her crew. A few Englishmen managed to make their way onto the breakwater and even to silence some of the cannons there, but they could go no farther against the overwhelming Spanish defense.

Meanwhile, some of the boats, including those carrying Troubridge and his men, had overshot the breakwater and capsized in the surf or been flung against the rocky shore. Unhurt himself, Troubridge rallied as many men as he could and made his way to the town square, only to be stopped there as his hapless compatriots had been on the breakwater.

During the hellish night seven British officers and 139 seamen and marines were killed and another 105 men wounded. Among the most severely wounded was Nelson himself. As he had drawn his sword in the assault on the breakwater, musket fire had shattered his right arm above the elbow. His men managed to get him back to the *Theseus*, where the arm was amputated.

*   *   *

The victors' treatment of the vanquished at Tenerife was courtly in the extreme. The governor of the island, Don Antonio Gutierrez, required only British assurance that there would be no more hostile action against Santa Cruz. That given, he allowed the invaders to return with their weapons to their ships; he even offered to lend them boats for transport if they lacked enough. Prisoners were released, and Englishmen too badly wounded to be moved were cared for in local hospitals. Boats were permitted to come ashore for provisioning, and Gutierrez himself sent wine and bread to his brave enemies "to refresh the people." Such generosity must have been hard to bear for Nelson, who could only try to reply in kind with the gift of a cask of English beer and some cheese.

Pain from his wounds—to his body and his pride—was terrible, and grief for the men lost because of his own rashness ran deep. The tactical blunders of assaulting a well-defended position with an inferior force and of underestimating his enemy were inexcusable and indefensible. On rejoining St. Vincent's fleet on August 16, Nelson scrawled a note to his superior, saying that a "left-handed Admiral will never again be considered as useful, therefore the sooner I get to a very humble cottage the better, and make room for a better man to serve the State."

But St. Vincent cast no blame. "Mortals cannot command success," the admiral wrote. "You and your Companions have certainly deserved it, by the greatest degree of heroism and perseverance that ever was exhibited."

That sentiment resounded throughout England as Nelson returned home to recuperate. If he had failed at Tenerife, at least he had failed with valor, and the empty sleeve pinned to the front of his uniform conferred absolution. He was now thirty-eight years old, his hair prematurely white, his body in agony from a wound failing to heal properly. But the British saw in his frail, battle-ravaged, but still-erect frame their own national image: gallantry against all odds. He was the living symbol of their pride and hope, and they took him to their hearts as they had no other hero.

There was irony in the fact that failure, not success, had brought him home to England to be the focus of such adulation at this particular time. With the government casting about for the right man to lead a Mediterranean expedition against Napoleon, there was no escaping the obvious: it must be Nelson.

If only Nelson could find him.

After Nelson lost his right arm, this combination knife and fork, rendered in gold with a steel cutting edge, was given to him by Lady Spencer, wife of the first lord of the Admiralty. The tactful gift followed a dinner party she hosted, at which Nelson's wife had to cut up his food for him.

THE BAND OF BROTHERS

"We few, we happy few, we band of brothers." The words are from Shakespeare's *Henry V*, part of the rousing speech wherein the young fifteenth-century English king tries to hearten his outnumbered men before their triumph over the French at Agincourt. Horatio Nelson, who knew his Shakespeare, borrowed from this stirring passage to describe his own captains at the Battle of the Nile. "I had the happiness to command a Band of Brothers," he wrote to Lord Howe after the victory, and he used the same phrase in letters to his wife and Earl St. Vincent.

The words did not necessarily imply a special fraternal feeling, for the Brothers came from different backgrounds and social strata, and not all were well acquainted with one another or with their admiral. But the phrase did convey a special pride that Nelson took in these men and a respect for the ability and mettle they showed at Aboukir Bay. His admiration has been shared by two centuries' worth of naval historians, who generally agree that no finer assemblage of officers ever fought at sea. In order of seniority, they were:

SIR JAMES SAUMAREZ, CAPTAIN OF THE *ORION*

The scion of a distinguished naval family in the Channel Islands, Saumarez was, because of seniority, second in command at the Nile. He was about two years older than Nelson, but although he was regarded as a thoroughly competent officer, he had not risen in the naval hierarchy as fast. As captain of a frigate, Saumarez fought a successful engagement against the French in 1793. He took command of the *Orion* two years later and was her captain in the Battle of Cape St. Vincent. Saumarez was not especially close to Nelson. The admiral seldom singled out this captain for special praise, and Saumarez was at times critical of his admiral's decisions and tactics. They differed greatly in style of command: Saumarez tended to be distant with his officers and men, inspiring none of the reverence that Nelson enjoyed. Nevertheless, the captain was sensitive to the burden his superior shouldered during the long search for Napoleon's armada. "Fortunately, I only act here *en second*," Saumarez wrote to his wife, "but did the chief responsibility rest with me, I fear it would be more than my too irritable nerves would bear." When higher command came his way later in his career, however, he met the challenge with distinction, leading the Baltic Fleet admirably from 1808 to 1812.

THOMAS TROUBRIDGE, CAPTAIN OF THE *CULLODEN*

If Nelson was somewhat wary of the well-born and rather formal Saumarez, he relied heavily on his next most senior captain, his long-time friend Thomas Troubridge, the plain-spoken son of a London baker. Troubridge first went to sea as a cabin boy in a merchantman, and later he and Nelson were midshipmen together on the frigate *Seahorse* in the West Indies. Promoted to captain early in 1783, Troubridge saw action during the American Revolution and took command of the *Culloden* in 1795. He fought gallantly at Cape St. Vincent and was Nelson's second in command in the abortive raid on Tenerife. Like two of his admirers, Nelson and Earl St. Vincent, Troubridge was forthright, scornful of subtlety, a relentless fighter and inspirational leader. In fact, St. Vincent, though Nelson's great patron, thought Troubridge the better officer, regarding him as nothing less than "the greatest man in that walk that the English navy has ever produced." Nelson was similarly effusive, calling him "the very best sea officer in His Majesty's Service." Sadly, the warm bond between Nelson and Troubridge before the Nile did not survive long after it. Like the honest friend he was, Troubridge was concerned about Nelson's behavior with Emma Hamilton, and his outspoken disapproval of the affair caused a rift that widened over the years.

Sir James Saumarez is depicted in this engraving by William Greatbach.

of the *Minotaur* in 1794. He and Nelson scarcely knew each other. He would serve with distinction after the Nile and be rewarded with a baronetcy.

JOHN PEYTON, CAPTAIN OF THE *DEFENCE*

The grandson of an admiral and son of an official of the Navy Office, Peyton also had three brothers in the navy. He had served on his grandfather's flagship in the American Revolution and was promoted to captain thereafter, commanding frigates under St. Vincent in the Mediterranean. Although ill at the time of the Nile campaign, he served ably.

ALEXANDER JOHN BALL, CAPTAIN OF THE *ALEXANDER*

The younger son of a Gloucestershire landowner, the urbane, charming, and highly intelligent Ball was a man of wide-ranging interests. Unlike many of his colleagues, he made use of his maritime travels to study the peoples and cultures of lands that he visited, and his understanding of diversity made him an adept manager of men. After he saved Nelson's flagship off Sardinia, displaying great valor and seamanship, Ball became one of the admiral's most intimate confidants. The captain had no family ties to the navy, but as a lieutenant in the American War of Independence he had won the favor of Admiral George Rodney, who sponsored his rise to commander and then captain. After the Nile, Ball would prove an excellent administrator on land, gaining renown as the highly effective colonial governor of Malta.

HENRY D'ESTERRE DARBY, CAPTAIN OF THE *BELLEROPHON*

Of Irish ancestry, Henry Darby was the nephew of a vice admiral who had been commander in chief of England's Channel Fleet in 1780. The captain had served against the French since the beginning of the revolutionary wars, but the glamourless nature of his duties—mostly escorting convoys—kept him inconspicuous. Darby was considered an able officer, if not a particularly gifted one; nevertheless, he fought with great bravery at the Nile, where the *Bellerophon* bore the brunt of the *Orient*'s wrath early in the battle.

THOMAS LOUIS, CAPTAIN OF THE *MINOTAUR*

Louis had served the Royal Navy as a lieutenant in the American Revolution but had not seen action since. He oversaw press-gangs in Ireland for a time before his appointment as captain

SAMUEL HOOD, CAPTAIN OF THE *ZEALOUS*

Of all the Band, Hood had the most impressive navy connections. Two of his cousins were admirals commanding major fleets, one of them the Samuel Hood whom Nelson had served under at Corsica. Hood served with both his cousins during the American Revolution, advancing to commander under Sir Samuel Hood. He was promoted to captain of the *Zealous* in 1796 and served at Tenerife with Nelson and Troubridge. His august family connections aside, Hood was a fine officer in his own right, and he loved life at sea. He was an avid student of many disciplines related to his work, among them astronomy, navigation, geography, shipbuilding, mechanics, and languages. He and Nelson were not close personal friends, but the admiral regarded Hood with respect.

DAVIDGE GOULD, CAPTAIN OF THE *AUDACIOUS*

Probably the least notable member of the Band, Gould was a good organizer and a dutiful officer, if not a distinguished one. He participated in several fleet actions but performed no deeds that made him especially memorable.

THOMAS FOLEY, CAPTAIN OF THE *GOLIATH*

If Gould was short on initiative and daring, Foley had plenty of it. It was he who shaped the victory at the Nile more than any other captain by leading part of Nelson's squadron inshore of the French at the battle's outset. The son of Welsh landowners, Foley was promoted to captain in 1790

This portrait of Capt. Thomas Foley late in his career is attributed to artist William Grimaldi.

and was flag captain under three admirals, one of them Sir John Jervis at the Battle of Cape St. Vincent. Jervis thought him competent, but it was not until the Nile that Foley made an indelible mark on naval history.

GEORGE BLAGDEN WESTCOTT, CAPTAIN OF THE *MAJESTIC*

Fifty-three at the time of the Nile, Westcott was by far the oldest member of the Band and was the only captain killed in the battle. Like Troubridge, his origins were lowly—his father was a baker from Devon and his brother a tailor—and little is known of his early service. Westcott probably came up through the ranks, and he was over thirty before he won his lieutenant's commission and forty-five when he was promoted to captain. However humble Westcott's beginnings, Nelson's friend Captain Cuthbert Collingwood described him as "a good officer and a worthy man."

BENJAMIN HALLOWELL, CAPTAIN OF THE *SWIFTSURE*

Hallowell was one of two American-born members of the Band, the son of a Boston customs official. He served with Nelson on Corsica, winning the future admiral's praise for "indefatigable zeal, activity, and ability." Hallowell also took part in the Battle of Cape St. Vincent, and he was appointed to the *Swiftsure* about a year later. A member of Nelson's favored inner circle, Hallowell was the captain who had had wood from the *Orient*'s mainmast fashioned into a coffin for his admiral. Nelson was amused and delighted with the gift, and he always kept it with him in his ship's cabin.

RALPH WILLET MILLER, CAPTAIN OF THE *THESEUS*

Miller was the other American-born Brother, the son of a Tory family in New York. He considered himself English and joined the Royal Navy to fight the American rebels. Like Hallowell, Miller won Nelson's approbation in action on Corsica, and Nelson appointed him his flag captain on the *Captain*, Nelson's ship at Cape St. Vincent. In 1797 he moved with Nelson to the *Theseus*, where he and the admiral were able to bring order and harmony to a crew infected by the mutiny that was rampant elsewhere in the British fleet at the time. As captain of the *Theseus*, Hallowell commanded one of the shore parties at Tenerife. He, too, was part of the admiral's inner circle, and Nelson once called him the only truly virtuous man he ever knew. Miller would be killed less than a year after the Nile in a battle off Acre.

THOMAS BOULDEN THOMPSON, CAPTAIN OF THE *LEANDER*

Thompson was another veteran of Tenerife; he knew the island well, and information he supplied about it was crucial to the operation's planning. He was the nephew of a navy man, Commodore Edward Thompson, whom he so admired that he adopted his surname.

THOMAS MASTERMAN HARDY, COMMANDER OF THE *MUTINE*

Of all the Brothers, Hardy was the one whose history would be linked most closely with Nelson's. He was the only one who would be with the admiral at his three greatest battles: the Nile, Copenhagen, and Trafalgar. Their friendship began when Hardy was a young lieutenant in the frigate *Minerve*, which Nelson served aboard briefly as commodore. The Nile came early in Hardy's career, but he had already impressed Nelson with his resourcefulness and courage. Among other feats, Hardy had commanded the boats that captured the French brig *Mutine* off Tenerife in 1797, and he was appointed her commander. He was expert in sensing Nelson's thoughts and moods and responding to them, and he became the admiral's favorite flag captain. That was the post Hardy held on the *Victory* at Trafalgar, and he was with the admiral until the hour of Nelson's death.

EDWARD BERRY, FLAG CAPTAIN OF THE *VANGUARD*

Another man after Nelson's own heart, the dashing Berry was a fierce and courageous fighter and also, according to his admiral, "a perfect gentleman in all his ideas, and one of the best and most gallant officers in our service." Ten years younger than Nelson, Berry was also from Norfolk. He served as Nelson's lieutenant on the *Agamemnon*, the ship he himself would command at Trafalgar. Nelson took Berry with him as first lieutenant on the *Captain*, and at Cape St. Vincent, Berry was the first to board the Spanish ship *San Nicolás* at the famous climax of the battle. Like several other members of the Band—among them Troubridge, Ball, Hallowell, Hardy, and Foley—Berry would rise to the rank of admiral in the years following the Battle of the Nile.

Sir Edward Berry, generally regarded as the handsomest of Nelson's captains, is captured in this portrait by John Singleton Copley.

The Battle of
the Nile

Previous page:
As Egyptian peasants watch
from the shore, the British squadron,
under full sail, speeds toward battle with
the French warships lying at anchor in
Aboukir Bay. Captain Thomas Foley's Goliath
is just rounding the head of the enemy line
in this Nicholas Pocock painting of the
Battle of the Nile's onset.

Above:
In a strong gale nimble sailors
struggle to reef their ship's topsails.
Reducing the area of canvas exposed
to the wind was crucial to keeping
a ship safe in a storm.

s Horatio Nelson's Mediterranean game of hide-and-seek with Bonaparte began, there seemed to be no doubt whom destiny favored: Napoleon, regally ensconced in the mighty *Orient*, sailed for Egypt confident of coming glory while Nelson battled just to save his ship.

His flag on the 74-gun *Vanguard*, the admiral had rendezvoused with the fleet of his old commander in chief, Earl St. Vincent, off Cádiz at the end of April 1798. St. Vincent was dispatching him to the inland sea, now virtually a French lake, with a reconnaissance force of three frigates and two more 74s—the *Orion*, captained by Sir James Saumarez, and the *Alexander*, under Captain Alexander Ball. The squadron was to sail for Toulon to find out what Bonaparte was planning.

The contingent was small, but its mission was crucial. It was well known that Napoleon had assembled a huge armada at Toulon and Genoa. The French sword might fall anywhere: on the Kingdom of Naples and Sicily, on Greece, on Gibraltar (England's last Mediterranean outpost), or on Egypt (threatening vital British trade with India). Now friendless in Europe but for the tepid support of Portugal, vulnerable England had to discover where the blow was aimed. Her very survival might depend on it.

On the night of May 8, Nelson's squadron sailed eastward along the French coast with fair winds. The ships were 75 miles south of Toulon on the evening of May 20 when, with little warning, gale-force winds howled out of the northwest, pushing huge swells before them. The *Vanguard* was hard hit. "On

Monday at half past one a.m., the main top-mast went over the side, as did the mizzen-top-mast soon afterwards," Nelson wrote. "About half past three o'clock the foremast went in three pieces, and the bowsprit was found to be sprung in three places." First light on Tuesday, May 22, found the British ships being pushed east-southeast toward the hostile coast of Corsica, and still the gale roared. Only by midafternoon was there enough of a lull for Nelson to signal the *Alexander* to take the wallowing *Vanguard* in tow.

With consummate seamanship, Captain Ball maneuvered his own ship and the stricken flagship east from Corsica toward the little Sardinian island of San Pietro. But the sea still rolled so heavily that for a time it appeared both ships would be dashed against the rocky shore, and Nelson called through the spindrift for Ball to cast the *Vanguard* loose and save his own ship. As his admiral doubtless would have done in such circumstances, Ball disobeyed, blithely ignoring all ensuing threats and curses. "I feel confident that I can bring you in safe," he shouted back. "I therefore must not and by the help of almighty God will not leave you." Nelson had met Ball briefly fifteen years earlier and thought him a bit of a fop, but henceforth the *Alexander*'s urbane captain would be one of his most trusted confidants.

Within hours, all three 74s were anchored safely in San Pietro Bay in the lee of the westerly swell. Ships' carpenters jury-rigged the *Vanguard* for sea in four days,

A painting by Italian artist Giacomo Guardi shows Nelson's fleet anchored in the Bay of Naples in June of 1798. The squadron was on a mission to borrow frigates and seek possible news of the whereabouts of Napoleon's elusive armada.

but Nelson's squadron now faced the fact that it would be searching for its quarry without eyes. The storm had separated the ships of the line from the three frigates, whose captains had headed for Gibraltar, believing Nelson would put in there for repairs.

On May 19, the day before the storm had began mauling the English squadron, the French armada had sailed from Toulon. By now it had passed serenely

through the Gulf of Genoa and proceeded south between Corsica and Italy, unmolested by man or nature.

*   *   *

Nelson headed back for Toulon in hopes of finding his frigates. They were still missing, but on June 5 the English brig *Mutine* hove into view, and its com-

mander, Thomas Masterman Hardy, brought good news. Under orders from the Admiralty, St. Vincent had dispatched ten additional 74s and the 50-gun *Leander* to join Nelson's squadron. Moreover, the new contingent was led by the *Culloden*, under Thomas Troubridge, Nelson's old shipmate and one of the navy's most respected captains. Commanding the other ships were men of similar quality, prompting Nelson to remark

No.1

The Rock of Gibraltar from the Spanish Lines.

No.2

The Devil's Tower.

No.3

CEUTA POINT, bearing S by E 3/4 East.

FRANCE

Bay of Biscay

SPAIN

Pyrenees

Barcelona

Carthagena

Cadiz

Andalusia

Gibralter

Ceuta

Tanger

Tetuan

I. Alboran

Oran

Algiers

Fez

AFR   ICA

C. de Gata

May 1798

Toulon

Hieres

Calvi

Corsica

I. Elba

Gorgona

Capraia

Leghorn

Lucca

Florence

Ancona

Orbitello

Rome

Ponza

Track of the British Fleet

Track of the French Fleet

Sardinia

St Pietro

Cagliari

June 1.

Majorca

Minorca

Iviça

June 1.

Track of the British Squadron Commanded by Commodore Troubridge which join'd Adm l Nelson off Toulon June 7th

Track of the British Fleet

Commanded by the Earl of St Vincent, forming the Blockade of Cadiz.

The British Fleet

May 23 1798

Lago di Garda

Trieste

Verona

Padua

Ferrara

Venice

Bologna

Apennines

Genoa

C. Bon

Ancient Carthage

Tunis

Pantelaria

Sicily

I. Ustica

Palermo

I. Maritimo

Gozzo

Mal

Tripoli

Meridian of Paris

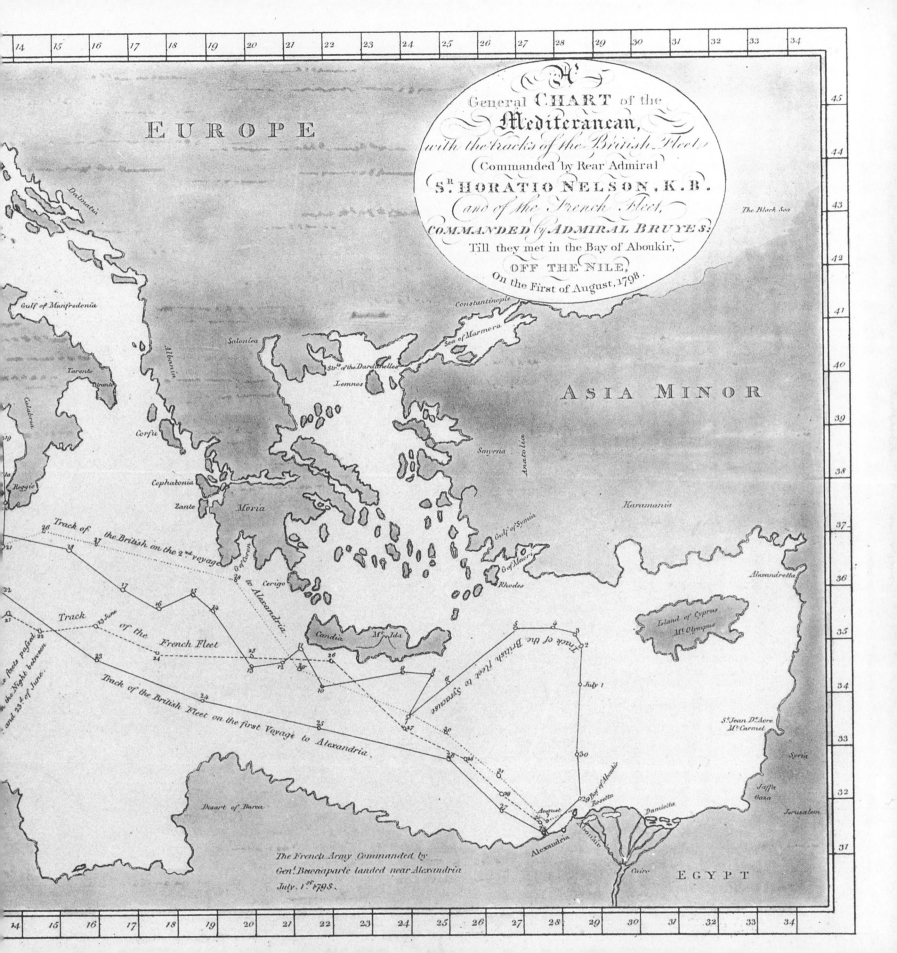

EUROPE

General CHART of the
Mediteranean,
with the tracks of the British Fleet
Commanded by Rear Admiral
Sr. HORATIO NELSON, K.B.
and of the French Fleet,
COMMANDED by ADMIRAL BRUYES:
Till they met in the Bay of Aboukir,
OFF THE NILE,
On the First of August, 1798.

The Black Sea

Dalmatia

Gulf of Manfredonia

Tarento

Constantinople

Saloniea

Str. of the Dardanelles

Sea of Marmora

Albania

ASIA MINOR

Corfu

Lemnos

Calabria

Smyrna

Anatolia

Karamania

Reggio

Cephalonia

Zante

Moria

Gulf of Syria

Alexandretta

Track of the British on the 2nd voyage

G. of Macri

Rhodes

Island of Cyprus
Mt. Olympus

Cerigo

Track of the French Fleet

to Alexandria

C. of Doron

Candia

Mt. Ida

July 1

St. Jean D'Acre
Mt. Carmel

Syria

Track of the British Fleet to Syracuse

Track of the British Fleet on the first Voyage to Alexandria

the fleets passed

the Night between

and 23d. of June

Jaffa
Gaza

Jerusalem

Desert of Barca

Bay of Aboukir
Rosetta

Damietta

August

Alexandria

Aboukir

The French Army Commanded by
Genl. Buonaparte landed near Alexandria
July 1st 1798.

Cairo

EGYPT

Previous page:
A contemporary map of
the Mediterranean tracks
the movements of the
French and British fleets
prior to the Battle of the
Nile. Toward the center is
the spot southeast of Sicily
where the enemy fleets
barely missed each other
before Admiral Brueys
veered to the northeast in
an evasive action.

that his new force would be "a match for any hostile fleet in the Mediterranean." And indeed, St. Vincent was sending his junior admiral the best he had, for the mission had changed: Nelson was now not only to find Napoleon but to stop him. On finding any part of the French armada, St. Vincent directed, "you are to use your utmost endeavors to take, sink, burn, or destroy it."

Troubridge's reinforcements joined Nelson on June 7, and by June 10 the squadron had checked Genoa and was proceeding southeast along the Italian coast to look into other ports. There was no sign of the French.

In fact, Napoleon was now at Malta. The island had fallen to him on June 12.

One day later Nelson learned from a Tunisian warship that the French had been seen off Sicily nine days earlier, heading east. From this the admiral surmised that if Bonaparte were indeed bypassing Sicily, his most probable destination was Egypt. Still unsure, however, he made for Naples and dispatched Troubridge to try to borrow some Neapolitan frigates. The nominally neutral Naples, fearing the French, refused him, but Sir William Hamilton did pass along news of Napoleon's attack on Malta. Nelson revised his thinking again: Malta was a direct stepping stone to Sicily. Still without scouts, he led his fleet down through the Strait of Messina and along Sicily's eastern coast, where all seem peaceful. Malta was now only about 70 miles to the south.

On the early morning of June 22, off Cape Passero,

Sicily's southeasternmost point, one of Nelson's vessels, the *Defence*, spotted four ships to the east-southeast. The *Leander* was sent to investigate. At about the same time, Hardy's *Mutine* intercepted a brig whose master, sailing from Malta, reported that the French had left there six days earlier, destination unknown. Nelson now concluded that since Sicily had not been attacked, the destination was almost surely Egypt. What he did not know was that the brig's master had been wrong about the timing: the French head start was only three days, not six. Without this crucial piece of information, the admiral failed to attach sufficient import to the *Leander*'s signal at 6:46 a.m. that the ships the *Defence* had spotted were frigates. Determined to keep his own ships together, Nelson directed the *Leander* to call off the search and rejoin the squadron. In any case, she could not have overtaken the smaller, faster vessels.

In fact, the frigates were French, the outlying edge of the armada itself. It was fewer than 30 miles away, lumbering along at the speed of its cumbersome troopships. Had he known this, Nelson could easily have overtaken it and had in his gunsights not only the French fleet but also a thirty-thousand-man army—and Napoleon himself. Within a few days a blood-drenched future might have changed for Europe.

But fortune smiled where she chose. Even as Nelson called a few of his most trusted captains aboard the *Vanguard* to discuss his decision to bear southeast, straight for Egypt, the paths of the adversaries were diverging.

Thus it was that on the *Orient*'s mist-shrouded quarterdeck that night, Admiral Brueys, detouring northward into the Ionian Sea, heard far off across the water the thud of cannons as the enemy ships sought to keep together in the night. His reckoning with the English was not yet at hand.

＊　　＊　　＊

Flying before favorable winds on a direct course, Nelson's ships arrived at Alexandria on June 28— only to find the ancient port empty of any sign of the French.

The admiral was now drowning in doubt: it seemed he had been wrong about Egypt. Napoleon had taken Malta and still eluded him, bound for God knew where. His nerves too taut to tolerate inaction, Nelson sailed east again on June 30 and then north, up past Syria toward Turkey.

Had he lingered on the Egyptian coast for only twenty-five more hours, he would have met the arriving French armada.

Finding Levantine waters empty, the desperate British turned back toward the west, skirting the southern coast of Crete (no French there, either) and fighting the wind en route to Sicily. On July 21 they put into Syracuse for water and provisions, allowing Nelson entirely too much time to ponder how it was possible that he had crossed the length of the Mediterranean and back without finding the enemy. Before leaving Syracuse he told his captains, "I now acquaint you that I shall steer direct for the Island of Cyprus, and hope in Syria to find the French fleet."

The British sailed east again on July 25. The day before, a victorious Napoleon, having defeated the Mamelukes at the Pyramids, had entered Cairo.

On the way to Cyprus, Captain Troubridge in the *Culloden* detoured briefly into the anchorage of Koroni on Greece's Peloponnesian coast to seek information. There he captured and took in tow a French wine brig, thus providing some pleasant vintage for the fleet. His news, though, was far headier. He had talked with a Turkish official, who reported that a month earlier the French armada had passed south of Crete, headed southeast.

It was Egypt after all.

＊　　＊　　＊

On the morning of August 1, two advance ships, the *Alexander* and the *Swiftsure*, arrived at Alexandria to find the French tricolor flying in the town and the harbor full of French merchantmen. But the French fleet was not there. Two more English vessels, the *Zealous* and *Goliath*, started cruising along the coast east of the city toward the only other likely anchorage: Aboukir Bay. At 2:45 p.m. the *Zealous* hoisted signal flags informing the admiral that the bay did indeed harbor the enemy: "sixteen sail of the line at anchor bearing East by South." A lieutenant on the *Goliath* made it "thirteen sail of the line, four large frigates and eight or ten corvettes." The *Orient*, he noted, was in the center.

On the French flagship, Admiral Brueys called a council of war to discuss his options. He did not want to fight; his primary job, after all, was to protect Napoleon's back and follow whatever orders the general gave. Shorthanded when they sailed, his ships were

A sailor lashed to his ship's bow "heaves the lead," measuring the water's depth with a lead-weighted line. This practice was crucial for preventing large vessels maneuvering close to shore from running aground. The British leadsmen were kept busy as their ships turned inshore of the French along the ill-charted coast of Aboukir Bay.

The sides were about equal, with thirteen ships of the line each. And nominally, at least, the French had more guns, a total of 1,026, although not all were mounted. The English vessels—the thirteen 74s and the *Leander*—bore only 938 cannons (though all these were fully operational, and many of the ships carried carronades as well). Brueys had deployed his vessels as best he knew how: standing stern to bow, close to shore, with gaps of perhaps 200 yards between them, they presented their starboard sides seaward in a fairly formidable wall. And there was further protection from the fort that guarded the entrance to Aboukir Bay. Besides, he would have time to recall his shore parties; the enemy ships could not reach him until nearly nightfall, so doubtless they would stand off until morning. Surely no commander would risk a night battle on an unfamiliar coast, with the dangers of sister ships firing on one another in the dark or running aground.

Or so the French admiral reasoned.

In fact, Nelson never hesitated. He had vowed to attack the French whenever and wherever he found them, and that is what he meant to do. It was now 2:30 p.m., and the enemy was about 9 miles away. The British ships were uncharacteristically scattered, the *Alexander* and *Swiftsure* perhaps 3 miles south of the main fleet toward Alexandria, the *Culloden* about 7 miles behind it with her wine brig in tow, the *Goliath* and *Zealous* eastward toward the enemy. The remaining ships were grouped randomly in a circle about 3 miles across.

now further undermanned. Thousands of sailors were onshore foraging for food or digging much-needed wells for the thirsty, hungry fleet that Napoleon had failed to resupply. They were protected by still more shipmates against local Bedouins who delighted in picking off the shore parties. Brueys thought about making for the open sea, then changed his mind.

Nelson wasted no time forming a tidy line of battle. He merely called in the outlying ships and signaled the entire fleet to prepare for battle and head for Aboukir Bay. That done, the admiral, who had eaten hardly anything for days, ordered and enjoyed a hearty meal. Shortly before 4:00 p.m. the ships began rounding the shoal at the bay's western end, unperturbed by the shore fort's cannons, which fired short. The British were now about 3 miles from the enemy.

* * *

By 5:30, when Nelson signaled, "form a battle line as most convenient," the *Goliath* and *Zealous*, closest to the French, were already jockeying for first position, enjoying a sailor's greatest ally, a favoring wind. Both ships were sounding as they went to determine the water depth along the coast. The *Goliath* won the race, which was probably just as well; her captain, Thomas Foley, had the best charts of the shore. It was also Foley who, in a sublimely inspired moment, gave the English an extraordinary advantage in the coming fight.

Only 200 yards from the head of the enemy line, he saw that the French ships rode on single anchors, attached to cables that seemed to measure the usual 240 yards. Nelson, on the *Vanguard*, apparently spotted this fact at nearly the same moment and, as though reading his captain's mind, exclaimed, "Where there is room for a French 74 at single anchor to swing, there is room for a British 74 to anchor."

With hardly any time for thought, Foley brought the *Goliath* inshore of the French, moving along a larboard

An engraving of Vice Admiral François Paul, Comte de Brueys d'Aigailliers, captures something of the French commander's proud fatalism. All but certain that his fleet at the Nile was doomed, he nevertheless fought gallantly to the end.

side that he knew must be unprepared and ill defended. It was Foley's genius that he spotted the weakness. It was Nelson's genius that his captain felt secure enough in the admiral's trust to exploit the opportunity.

The setting sun gilding their sails, four more British ships followed the *Goliath* inshore: the *Zealous*, *Audacious*, *Orion*, and *Theseus*. As they went, all loosed raking fire at the hapless *Guerrier*, the first ship of the weak French van, completely dismasting her in the first ten minutes of battle. Nevertheless, she fought back, firing at each ship that passed. Foley had intended to anchor next to her but overshot his mark and ended up midway between the second and third French ships, the *Conquérant* and *Spartiate*. Hood in the *Zealous* took up Foley's intended position opposite the wounded *Guerrier*, and next the *Audacious* under Captain Davidge Gould swung around the *Zealous* to move between the *Guerrier* and *Conquérant*.

This lively oil painting portrays the beginning of the action, seen from Nelson's position in the middle of the British line. His flagship Vanguard *(center) would later begin the British pincer movement down the outside of the French line.*

Maneuvering toward the fourth French ship, the *Aquilon*, Sir James Saumarez's *Orion* met with an unexpected distraction. A French frigate, the *Sérieuse*, riding shoreward of the battle line, fired on her. Frigates were ordinarily noncombatants, and it was deemed very bad form for a ship of the line to shoot at one. But by her action the *Sérieuse* had nullified that courtesy, and now she dared to move closer to the *Orion*. "Sink the brute," said Saumarez, and with that he coolly loosed a broadside at the plucky little ship, dismasting her and holing

her hull. She sank shortly thereafter.

Now the last ship to come inshore of the line, Captain Ralph Miller's *Theseus* moved toward the gap between the *Zealous* and the *Guerrier*, trusting that Captain Hood's gunners would hold their fire while she passed. They did, and the two British crews exchanged hearty cheers as their ships swept within 10 feet of each other. The crewmen of the *Guerrier* tried to counter with a cheer of their own, but it was a feeble effort. The *Theseus* moved inshore of the *Audacious* and *Goliath* to anchor alongside the *Spartiate*.

By now it was nearly nightfall, and the *Vanguard* was approaching. Nelson, seeing the inshore waters already crowded with his own ships, decided to move in seaward of the French, expecting that the vessels behind him— six 74s and the 50-gun *Leander*—would follow. The *Vanguard* anchored along the starboard side of the *Spartiate*, which was already being blasted on her larboard side by the *Theseus*. With Nelson's arrival, Captain Miller turned his bow fire on the next French ship, the *Aquilon*.

Now, following their admiral, the rest of the British ships turned toward the prey in graceful unison. The *Minotaur* pulled alongside the *Aquilon*, and the *Defence* anchored by the fifth French ship, the *Peuple Souverain*. The *Bellerophon* found herself beside the awesome bows of the *Orient*. The *Swiftsure* moved in just ahead, at the stern of the 80-gun *Franklin* (named for the American revolutionary who as ambassador had endeared himself to the French). Captain Ball's *Alexander* stationed herself at the *Orient*'s stern.

Next came the *Majestic*, which seemed to aim at the first French ship unengaged thus far, the 80-gun *Tonnant*, aft of the *Orient*. But something went wrong with the *Majestic*'s anchor cable; she ran past the *Tonnant* and into the next enemy vessel, the 74-gun *Heureux*, her bowsprit snarling itself in the French ship's rigging. Before the *Majestic* could disentangle herself, her captain, fifty-three-year-old George Westcott, was killed by musket fire and his ship was savaged, taking fire at point-blank range while her position prevented bringing her own guns to bear.

And there was more misfortune for the British. A little after 3 p.m., the *Culloden* had cast off the French wine brig she was towing and hurried toward the battle behind the rest of the fleet, making good time. But in rushing to catch up with his comrades, Captain Troubridge swung too near the shore—and ran aground on a shoal. Frustrated, furious, and mortified, the most aggressive of Nelson's captains would have to sit out the fight.

The only remaining English ship, the midsized *Leander*, seemed unsure whether to behave in battle as a frigate or a man-of-war. She did both, going first to the *Culloden*'s aid and then bravely stationing herself across the bows of the *Franklin*, flailing away at the bigger ship with her puny armament as best she could.

Foley's *Goliath* had fired the first shots of the battle at 6:28 p.m. It was 9:00 or 9:30 before the *Leander* joined the fray, but by then the twelve English 74s had long since deployed themselves fully, sandwiching the French line's van between their two ranks. Aboukir Bay had become a cauldron of smoke and thunder. Night enveloped Egypt's shore, but flashes of cannon fire riddled the moon-silvered dark as the battle settled into its relentless, lethal rhythm.

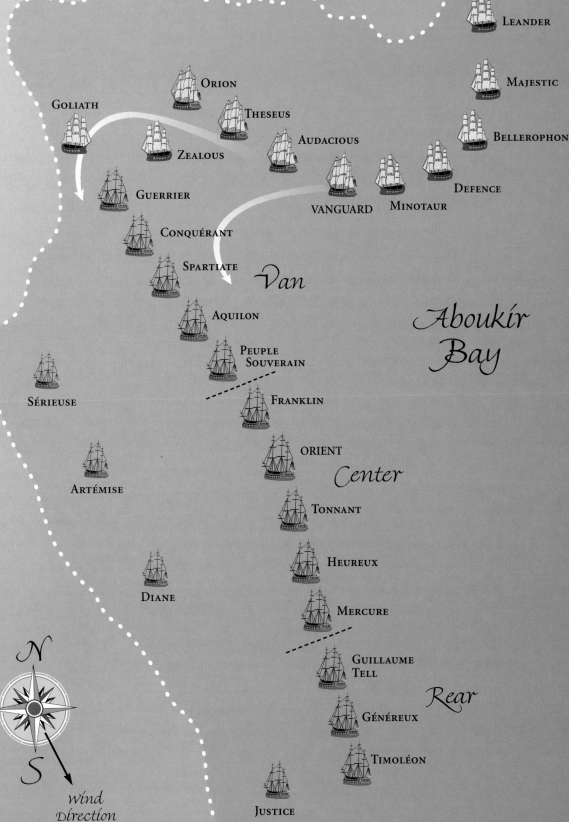

4 Fathom Line

CULLODEN

LEANDER

MAJESTIC

BELLEROPHON

ORION

THESEUS

GOLIATH

AUDACIOUS

DEFENCE

ZEALOUS

VANGUARD   MINOTAUR

GUERRIER

This map shows Admiral Nelson's squadron beginning to move into position against the French ships anchored along the shore of Aboukir Bay at the outset of the Battle of the Nile.

The leading British ship, Captain Thomas Foley's *Goliath*, has just moved across the bows of the French *Guerrier*, surprising the enemy by heading down its vulnerable shoreward side.

The *Goliath* would be followed by the *Zealous*, *Orion*, *Theseus*, and *Audacious*, while Nelson in the *Vanguard* would lead the next six English ships of the line down the seaward side.

(The *Culloden*, which ran aground, would not take part in the battle.)

Sandwiching the vessels of the French van between them, the two British lines would soon force them to surrender.

CONQUÉRANT

SPARTIATE

Van

AQUILON

Aboukir Bay

PEUPLE SOUVERAIN

SÉRIEUSE

FRANKLIN

ORIENT

Center

ARTÉMISE

TONNANT

HEUREUX

DIANE

MERCURE

GUILLAUME TELL

Rear

GÉNÉREUX

TIMOLÉON

JUSTICE

N

S

wind Direction

Turning across the head of the French van, the Goliath looses deadly raking fire at the Guerrier. A Goliath midshipman quoted Captain Foley as saying prophetically just before he made the turn "that he should not be surprised to find the Frenchmen unprepared for action on the inner side."

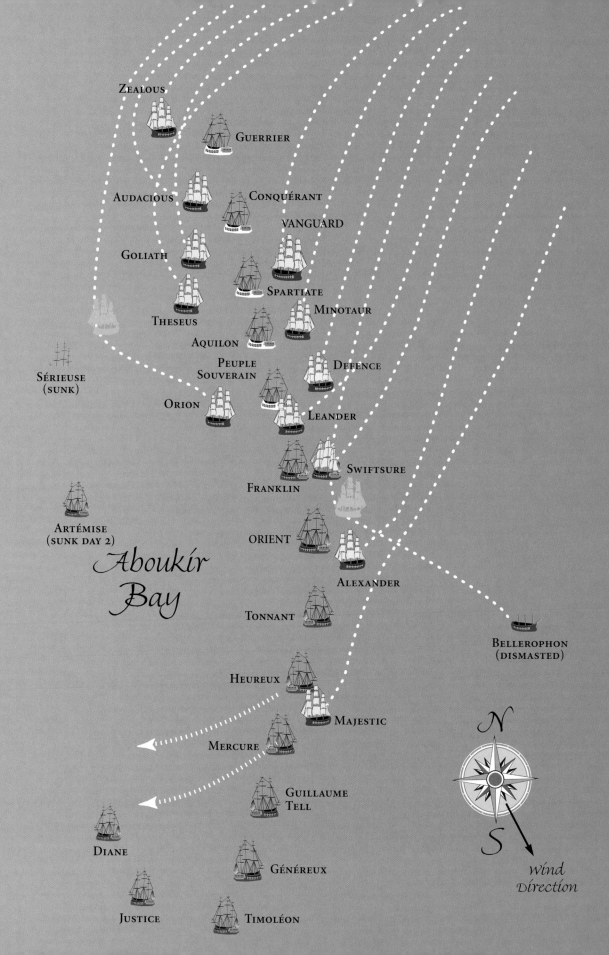

This map shows the deployment of Admiral Nelson's ships and the positions of the opposing British and French fleets during the first phase of the Battle of the Nile, prior to the explosion of the French flagship Orient.

Taking fire from both sides, the first five ships of the French line have by now surrendered.

Shoreward of them, the French frigate Sérieuse has sunk, holed by cannon fire from the Orion.

Farther down the battle line, the British ship Bellerophon, dismasted by the Orient, wears away from the fight and drifts seaward.

Trying to escape the impending explosion of the Orient, the French ships Heureux and Mercure have cut their anchor cables. As the arrows indicate, both ships will run aground, although they will continue firing from their stranded positions on the shoals when the battle resumes.

Astern of the Mercure are the only two French men-of-war to escape the Battle of the Nile, the Guillaume Tell and Généreux.

Ghosted ships: Orion sinks Sérieuse; Bellerophon dismasted by Orion.

ZEALOUS

GUERRIER

AUDACIOUS

CONQUÉRANT

VANGUARD

GOLIATH

SPARTIATE

MINOTAUR

THESEUS

AQUILON

DEFENCE

PEUPLE
SOUVERAIN

SÉRIEUSE
(SUNK)

ORION

LEANDER

SWIFTSURE

FRANKLIN

ARTÉMISE
(SUNK DAY 2)

Aboukir
Bay

ORIENT

ALEXANDER

TONNANT

BELLEROPHON
(DISMASTED)

HEUREUX

MAJESTIC

MERCURE

GUILLAUME
TELL

DIANE

GÉNÉREUX

JUSTICE

TIMOLÉON

N

S

Wind
Direction

LEGEND

ENGLISH
SHIP

FRENCH
SHIP

SURRENDERED
FRENCH SHIP

* * *

The French had been caught utterly unawares by the English movement down their inshore side. On some of their ships, the larboard gun ports were blocked by spare equipment and other gear that had been hastily piled on the shoreward side as the English approached, and this had to be cleared away before cannons could even be positioned to reply to the attackers. The weakest ships, those in the van, were the ones subjected to the worst pounding as the British moved in. Their shorthanded crews—all too many of them conscripted coastal fishermen or sailors trained mainly for transport duty, many of them sick, all of them hungry—were no match for the polished English gunners.

But they fought gallantly. Hit first and often by raking fire—shots that entered at the bows and skittered along a ship's length, hurling up deadly splinters that tore into flesh and bone—the *Guerrier* suffered terrible losses at the beginning of the battle. Still she refused to surrender. "I could not get *Le Guerrier*'s commander to strike for three hours," wrote Captain Hood of the *Zealous*, "though I hailed him twenty times, and seeing he was totally cut up and only firing a stern gun now and then at the *Goliath* and *Audacious*." In any case, the *Guerrier* had no colors to strike and no captain to strike them; the captain was dead, and the masts that would have borne the tricolor had gone over

the side minutes after the fight began. "At last being tired of firing and killing people in that way," Hood reported, "I sent my boat on board her, and the lieutenant was allowed . . . to hoist a light and haul it down to show his submission."

Astern of the *Guerrier*, the lieutenant commanding the weather-beaten and lightly armed *Conquérant* appeared more pragmatic. His decks already slimed with the blood of his men, he lowered his flag twelve minutes into the contest. Earlier, his wounded captain had been taken below decks, leaving an order to continue

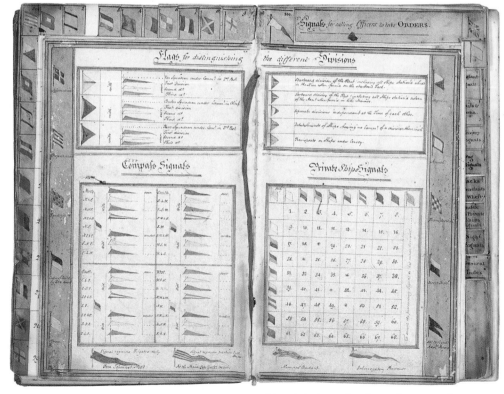

These pages are from a signal book believed to have been used during the Nile campaign. Signaling in the Royal Navy was not very evolved at the time, a problem Nelson countered both by briefing his captains on his battle plans in advance and by delegating authority for them to use their own initiative.

In the cockpit of the Vanguard, *Admiral Nelson is treated for his head wound. (The artist incorrectly amputated Nelson's left arm rather than the right). The wounded sailor on the right in this Matthew Dubourg engraving may be Richard Crader, a young ordinary seaman who had suffered a broken leg and was the first man taken to the cockpit for treatment.*

THE CARNAGE OF THE COCKPIT

The treatment of battle wounds was a very primitive art in Nelson's day, and shipboard surgeons were seldom men at the top of their profession. For these reasons—and because eighteenth-century sea warfare was such a body-mangling horror—a ship's cockpit during battle was apt to be a bedlam of blood and screams.

The usual treatment for a badly damaged limb was amputation, such as the one Nelson himself underwent after a musket ball shattered his right arm at Tenerife. His chief memory of the operation was the coldness of the knife, and thereafter he ordered surgeons to warm their knives before operating. Surgery was excruciating—there was no anesthetic—but the aftermath could be almost as bad. In Nelson's case a silk ligature used to tie off a bleeding artery grew into the wound and festered there, and he was in agony until the silk finally rotted and fell off.

At the Battle of the Nile, the surgeon's log of the *Vanguard* recorded a number of terrible injuries, most to the arms and legs and requiring amputation. Some not entailing the knife were nevertheless terrible; one John Triff, for example, a twenty-five-year-old able seaman, sustained a head wound that laid his skull bare and knocked out his right eye. Twenty-eight men had been treated or were still receiving aid in the cockpit by the time Nelson was brought down. Even though he believed he was dying, he insisted on observing the convention in this part of the ship that rank did not matter. "I will await my turn with my brave followers," he said.

No witness wrote an account of any ship's cockpit during the battle, but scenes on the more badly stricken ships must have resembled one reported by a surgeon at the Battle of Camperdown less than a year earlier. "Ninety wounded were brought down during the action," he wrote. "The whole cockpit, deck, cabins, wing berths, and part of the cable tier, together with my platform and my preparations for dressing, were covered with them. So that for a time they were laid on each other at the foot of the ladder where they were brought down.

"Joseph Bonheur had his right leg taken off by a cannon shot close to the pelvis, so that it was impossible to apply a tourniquet; his right arm was also shot to pieces. The stump of the thigh, which was very fleshy, presented a dreadful and large surface of mangled flesh. In this state he lived for near two hours, perfectly sensible and incessantly calling out in a strong voice to me to assist him."

The doctor went on to write of the "melancholy cries for assistance" from the wounded and dying on all sides, and of the "piteous moans and bewailing from pain and despair."

the fight. But only a few cannons were still firing, while the Frenchman's fragile old hull was under bombardment from the *Goliath* and *Audacious*. The latter's Captain Gould, who accepted the surrender, wrote that the carnage had been "so dreadful in the ship that the French officers declared it was impossible to make the men stand at their guns." There had been fewer than 400 men aboard the vessel, whose usual complement was more than 700. In the opening minutes of battle, at least 120 were killed and another 85 or 90 wounded.

There were more than 200 casualties aboard the *Spartiate*, the first ship in the French line to take fire from both sides. She lost two of her masts but suffered worse from the body blows: the *Vanguard* had put forty-nine holes in her starboard hull, the *Theseus* twenty-seven to larboard. Most of her surviving men had to be called away from the guns to man the ship's pumps. Even so, the *Spartiate* inflicted casualties aboard both her tormentors, and she held out for two hours before surrendering to Nelson's flagship. Shortly thereafter, the next ship in line, the *Aquilon*, surrendered to the *Minotaur*, and then the *Peuple Souverain* hauled down her colors.

There was probably no linkage in the cascade of surrenders. In the clamorous, smoke-thickened darkness, each ship was a self-contained hell, her men deafened by the cannons' boom and blind to the larger canvas of destruction beyond their particular wooden walls. On Nelson's orders, the British ships had hoisted lines of lanterns on their mizzen-tops; but these were only to minimize the risk of damage from friendly fire, not to illuminate the grotesqueries of battle. Had any man

been granted an Olympian view of the conflict, however, he would seen the French van being steadily and systematically crushed.

* * *

The chief author of this destruction, Admiral Nelson was forced to learn about much of it secondhand. A little after 8 o'clock, Nelson was standing with Captain Berry on the *Vanguard*'s quarterdeck when he was struck on the right side of his forehead by a piece of langrage shot fired from the *Spartiate*. An evil jumble of nails, bolts, chain, and other bits of iron tied together to form a cylinder, langrage was designed for cutting up enemy sail and rigging. Now it tore a three-inch gash in the admiral's flesh, laying the skull bare for about an inch. A flap of skin fell over Nelson's one good eye. Blinded, stunned, and severely concussed, he believed he was dying. "I am killed," he said to Berry, who caught him as he fell. "Remember me to my wife."

Seamen carried him down three ladderways to the ship's surgery, the red-painted cockpit, where a number of wounded were already being treated. It was tradition that rank had no standing in the cockpit, and Nelson insisted on waiting his turn. Even so, surgeon Michael Jefferson got to him promptly and found that the wound, while painful and ugly, was not mortal. He brought its edges together, applied liniment, dressed it with sticking plaster and lint, and ordered Nelson to the nearby bread room to rest—a command that, characteristically, the admiral found intolerable. He summoned his secretary and began dictating a letter to the

Admiralty while waiting for Berry to report on the battle. The captain came soon, and with good news. The *Aquilon* had struck her colors. The *Peuple Souverain* had surrendered.

Berry left but returned sometime thereafter with a report that prompted Nelson to insist on being helped back up to the quarterdeck. There was fire on board the *Orient*.

*   *   *

Despite the carnage farther up the line, the *Orient* herself had fared well in the early part of the battle. The first English ship to come under her guns was the *Bellerophon*, and she had suffered horribly for her effrontery. Overwhelmingly outgunned, Captain Henry Darby's ship lost two of her masts almost at once, and by the time she was forced to pull away from the duel, two hundred of her men—almost a fourth of the night's casualties for the entire British fleet—had been killed or wounded.

But like tenacious bulldogs, other English vessels had thrown themselves at the giant flagship. The *Swiftsure* pulled up at her bows and the *Alexander* abaft, pummeling her vulnerable stern. It was the devastating fire from the *Swiftsure* that killed Admiral Brueys.

Early in the battle Brueys had been wounded in the head and lost both his legs. When his men tried to take him below decks, he refused to go. "A French admiral must die on his quarterdeck," he said. And there he stayed, propped in a chair, tourniquets applied to the bloody stumps of his legs. He was still giving orders

The Orient *burns toward her final fate in this painting by an eyewitness, the Reverend Cooper Willyams, chaplain of the* Swiftsure. *Willyams would later write how the flagship "blew up with a crashing sound that deafened all around her. The tremendous motion, felt to the very bottom of each ship, was like that of an earthquake. The fragments were driven such a vast height into the air that some moments elapsed before they could descend."*

when shot from the *Swiftsure* almost cut him in two.

At least the commander of the French fleet was spared witnessing the fate of his ship, although he might well have surmised what lay in store. His last orders governed efforts to put out a fire in the *Orient*'s stern.

Shot from the *Alexander* had ignited the blaze in the flagship's cabin, and it spread quickly, fed, some said, by cans of paint and oil that crewmen had failed to clear from the afterdeck. As flames began to lick at the mizzen-chains, Captain Benjamin Hallowell in the *Swiftsure* made certain that it would not be extinguished. He ordered that every available cannon, along with the muskets of his marines, train their sights on the glowing target and kill any man who got near it. The tactic was devastatingly effective, and the conflagration soon howled out of control.

By this lurid beacon both British and French could assess the progress of the battle thus far and see that the entire French van had been subdued. But neither side had the leisure to contemplate the implications. It was clear that at any time the flames would reach the *Orient*'s magazines and the tons of gunpowder stored there. French or English, the ships scrambled to get out of the way.

In the *Alexander*, lying just astern, Captain Ball ordered his anchor cable cut, saving the hour it would have taken to raise it, and his ship began drifting down the French line. The *Bellerophon*, her masts either gone or useless, set sails on their stumps. About 300 yards from the *Orient*,

The fire rapidly spreads to the mighty Orient*'s powder magazines. Artist Thomas Hellyer captures the hellishness of the French flagship's demise in his rendering of the Battle of the Nile's climactic moments.*

Captain Saumarez had the *Orion*'s guns run in and her gun ports closed to prevent the coming inrush of super-heated air. He also shut down her magazine and ordered that all sail—highly flammable—be hauled down and stored below. Three French ships cut their cables: the *Tonnant*, *Heureux*, and *Mercure*. The *Tonnant* began moving rearward down the French line, where her sister ships were letting out cable so wind and current could carry them a few hundred yards farther away from their flagship. The other two unmoored Frenchmen, the *Heureux* and *Mercure*, soon ran aground.

As the various vessels effected what preparations they could, only the *Swiftsure*, closest to *Orient*, made no move to leave, even though heat was melting the tar between her planks. Captain Hallowell, posting sentries to keep any desperate crewmen from trying to cut the anchor chain, mustered water buckets and wet swabs and had his men take cover and wait. He reasoned, correctly, that his position just beneath her bows would offer his own ship the best protection against the concussion and fallout from the floating bomb the *Orient* had become.

By now her decks were littered with blazing corpses, and her remaining officers and men were jumping overboard, many of them naked, their clothes seared away by heat or flame. And the English, even while struggling to save their own ships, put out boats to pick them up. The sea had its ancient code: French or not, these enemies were sailors. As they struggled onboard the British ships, English seamen here and there took

Demonstrating humanity in the midst of devastation, English sailors rescue French survivors as the Orient *explodes. The painting is by English artist Arnald George.*

139

off their own shirts or jackets and helped the Frenchmen cover themselves. There were only a few: of the thousand seamen who had sailed on the *Orient*, about sixty survived. Nevertheless, on some British decks English and French watched together and in equal awe as the bomb finally exploded.

Rocked by the **Orient**'s *explosion, French seamen scramble frantically, often in vain, to cling to nearby ships. The vessel in the foreground of the Mather Brown painting is probably the* **Tonnant,** *which was anchored astern of the doomed French flagship.*

Shortly after 10 p.m. there was a roaring blast that shook every ship in the bay to her keel and was palpable far inland. Where the *Orient* had been, a colossal fireball bloomed and soared, visible a dozen miles away. Flung up within it were planks and masts and spars and rigging, tatters of flaming sail, chunks of human flesh—all that remained of what had been, a moment before, the pride of the French fleet. She was gone utterly.

After her cataclysmic death knell, an even eerier lament pervaded the scene of battle. Silence.

* * *

Afterward, no one could say with certainty how long the odd hiatus lasted. The captains' logs differed: three minutes, ten, fifteen, thirty, even an hour. During the lull, however, all firing ceased. It was as though every man in Aboukir Bay, regardless of allegiance, had been stunned into immobility by the magnitude of the destruction, the completeness of it.

Eventually, though, the battle sputtered back to life. The five English ships that had initially come in shoreward

of the French were virtually undamaged. Of the seaward line, all but the *Bellerophon* were still able to fight, although the *Majestic* had been badly mauled and the others battered to some degree.

The French, of course, had fared far worse. Of her first six ships, all had surrendered except the *Franklin*, and she had lost two of

Given the awful drama of the scene, the destruction of the Orient *was a popular theme for late-eighteenth-century artists. While some paintings dwelled on the human terror of the event, others, such as this one by John Thomas Serres, emphasized its sheer physical violence.*

her masts. Astern of her, now that the *Orient* had disappeared, the *Tonnant* was mastless and her gallant captain dead. (Admiral Aristide Aubert Dupetit-Thouars had unknowingly mimicked his own commander. With both arms and one leg shot away, he had ordered his men to prop him up in a bran tub, and there he continued with his duties for the short time it took him to bleed to death.) The *Heureux* and *Mercure*, though still capable of firing, were both aground. Only at the rear of the French line did three men-of-war remain undamaged, having taken no part in the battle: the *Timoléon*, *Généreux*, and *Guillaume Tell*.

The *Franklin* was the first French ship to resume firing after the *Orient's* explosion, pelting the *Defence* and *Swiftsure*. But her captain was badly wounded, two-thirds of her crew wounded or killed, and only three of her lower-deck cannons still capable of firing. After a short time she struck her colors.

Still, the *Franklin's* valor seemed to rally some of the remnants of the French fleet. Though grounded, the *Heureux* and *Mercure* began firing, along with the *Timoléon*, dueling futilely with the *Majestic* and *Alexander*

A dismasted hulk, the 80-gun Tonnant nevertheless held out for three days before surrendering at the end of the battle. Her crew was inspired by grief and vengeance at the death of her valiant captain, Admiral Aristide Aubert Dupetit-Thouars (inset). With both arms and one leg shot away, Dupetit-Thouars ordered his men to prop him in a bran tub so he could continue directing his men. His death is depicted at the lower left of the lithograph.

far into the night while other English ships gradually moved down to join in. The *Tonnant* was also still firing. But the action was ragged and confused. By now the formidable enemy against both sides was fatigue; men were dropping on deck or at their guns not from wounds but exhaustion. Nevertheless, as dawn broke, the fighting continued, though the two ships on the shoals eventually struck their colors.

At the rear of the French line, aboard the *Guillaume Tell*, Rear Admiral Pierre-Charles de Villeneuve had wrestled throughout the night with indecision. Admiral Brueys had deployed him at the rear because that was where an attack seemed likely but had left no orders about what to do in case the reverse happened. Villeneuve might have gone forward to help his beleaguered sister ships, but that would have meant leaving his post. He was a traditional, disciplined, dutiful, and quite unimaginative officer. In the end he stayed where he was, and for that, the hint of cowardice would haunt him for the rest of his life.

As the second day of battle wore on, he had to decide whether to fight or to try to escape, taking with him what ships he could as the nucleus for a force that might fight the British at a later date. He hailed the *Timoléon*, which was dismasted but still afloat and firing, and asked the captain's plans. Captain Trullet answered

that he would fight as long as he could and then set his ship on fire.

"Bravo!" Villeneuve shouted, but he himself had chosen another course. Just before midday the *Guillaume Tell*, *Généreux*, and two frigates cut loose their anchors and sped northeast out of Aboukir Bay, headed for Malta. Nelson, dazed and hurting but now back in action, signaled for the *Zealous* to give chase, but he soon called her back. Hood was willing, but his ship's rigging was damaged, and pursuit of the unscathed

Frenchmen was clearly futile. (Both the escaping warships would be captured in the Mediterranean within months, but in the battle's aftermath their flight pained Nelson more than his wound, marring a victory that was otherwise all but complete. He would write rather apologetically to St. Vincent about the four ships that "I am sorry to say made their escape; nor was it, I assure you, in my power to prevent them. Captain Hood had most handsomely endeavoured to do it, but I had no Ship in a condition to support *Zealous*, and I was obliged to call her in.")

Incredibly, the *Tonnant* and *Timoléon* held out for the rest of the day on August 2. When a boat from the *Theseus* approached to ask whether she would surrender, the *Tonnant* answered by training her guns on it. Valiant as they were, though, the French ships were by now little more than a nuisance, and the British concerned themselves mainly with repairing their own vessels and securing their prizes. The next morning Nelson dispatched the *Theseus* and *Leander* to deal with the *Tonnant*. Her captain first vowed to fight to the end but finally, realizing his position was quite hopeless, surrendered.

After the battle, Admiral Nelson held a prayer service on the Vanguard *to give thanks for the victory. He suggested that the other English ships hold similar ceremonies, although most of them lacked chaplains.*

In the *Timoléon*, Captain Trullet was true to his word. He had cut his cable, run his ship aground, and evacuated her men. Now a few remaining crewmen set her ablaze.

The Battle of the Nile—by any standard the most decisive triumph in the annals of war at sea—was over. But as they gazed around at the detritus of battle, at dismasted ships and burning hulks and the pool of debris that had once been the mighty *Orient*, some of the British must have realized even without history's insight that naval warfare had been redefined here.

Time was when a few colors struck, some prizes taken, a ship sunk here and there were enough for a side to declare victory. At the Nile, however, Nelson and his Band of Brothers had expanded the parameters to include another sort of outcome. They had proved that virtual annihilation was possible, an end to be sought.

VICTORS OF THE NILE

Mementos of the triumph in Aboukir Bay included an etching (left) called Victors of the Nile. Against a background of ships, smoke, and pyramids, Nelson's portrait is located midway in the trunk of a palm tree. Below it are cameo portraits of his fourteen captains, arranged in order of seniority, left to right and top to bottom.

EPILOGUE

One of the two French ships of the line that escaped from Aboukir Bay, the Guillaume Tell *made her way to Malta, which was under a British blockade after the Nile. Later, trying to run the blockade, she was captured by Captain Edward Berry in the* Foudroyant. *(Nelson himself should have been commanding the blockading fleet, but he was in Palermo with Emma. He had already captured the* Généreux, *the other escapee, and taking the* Guillaume Tell *would have been the crowning touch to his victory at the Nile.)*

"THE CATASTROPHE of Aboukir came like a thunderbolt on the General in Chief," according to Bonaparte's secretary, Louis Bourrienne, and even that remark could be called an understatement. General Kléber's messengers from Alexandria—now thronged with thousands of wounded, shipless sailors—reached his commander only on August 13. Until then Bonaparte had claimed and perhaps believed in a golden future for his Egyptian venture. In Cairo he had swiftly organized a central government, administered from his own headquarters in a splendid city palace. He had established his scholars—now known collectively as the Institute of Egypt in a series of mansions at the edge of the city. So confident was he that he had asked the Directory to send colonists, including the wives of his soldiers, troupes of actors, dancers, and puppeteers, and "fifty gardeners with their families and the seeds of every kind of vegetable."

This was overly optimistic, considering the realities even before the Battle of the Nile. Egypt was by no means pacified.

Gustave Bourgain's nineteenth-century water-color Napoleon in Cairo, 1798, *evokes an Orientalist's dream of the exotic setting while emphasizing the lonely burden borne by the commander. Within three days of entering the city, Bonaparte reorganized its government, appointing a council of local officials responsible only to him; similar administration was planned for every province.*

The Mameluke armies had withdrawn, but they would certainly return. Meanwhile, French troops outside Cairo could expect lightning attacks from Bedouin tribes and angry peasants. In only two months, seven thousand troops had died, victims of ambush, battle, thirst, and diseases ranging from dysentery to syphilis and gonorrhea; many were blinded by the purulent opthalmia endemic in the region. Sick, unhappy, under-fed, and underpaid, isolated in an ugly, hostile desert, the army was near mutiny. The soldiers—and their commanders—wanted only to go home.

The Battle of the Nile and the blockade that Nelson left behind made that impossible. As Bonaparte told his secretary, "We were now cut off from all communication with France and all hope of returning thither, except by a degrading capitulation with an implacable and hated enemy." There was no practicable way out of Egypt. Nor was there a way in for desperately needed reinforce-ments, supplies, and money.

In fact, small ships could run Nelson's blockade with messages, and Bonaparte took advantage of this oppor-tunity to rewrite history. As Bourrienne put it, his mas-ter "never hesitated to disguise the truth when he could make it embellish his own glory. He considered it sheer stupidity not to do so." During the year he remained in Egypt, Bonaparte's messages home reached matchless heights of invention.

There was first the loss of his entire fleet to explain. He did so by blaming the hapless Admiral Brueys, who he said had disobeyed his orders to enter the safe port of Alexandria or—if that proved impossible—to sail to Corfu. As Napoleon himself had earlier reported, it was

not possible to enter the port. Brueys's orders had been for the fleet to anchor at Aboukir Bay, leaving only if threatened by "a very superior force," which Nelson's was not. In any case, Brueys could not have sailed with-out water and food, and his pleas for these had been ignored.

In Egypt itself, Bonaparte's policy was unbelievable and unbelieved. He modified it according to the situa-tion. At the start of the venture, he had warned his troops that pillage, rape, and desecration of mosques were punishable by death. By July he was writing, "We have had to treat them [the Egyptians] gently so far as to destroy the reputation for brutality that preceded us: but today we must adopt the tone necessary to make these people obey, and, for them, to obey is to fear."

By autumn he was using fear as a weapon. Always proclaiming himself the friend of Egypt and of Islam—he even hinted at conversion—he instituted a range of forced loans and taxes to replenish his treasury. These were not popular with the Cairenes, still unreconciled to the invasion of infidels. In October, after word filtered in that the Ottoman Empire had declared war on France, part of the city rose in rebellion. It took two days for the French artillery and cavalry to control the insurrection, destroy Cairo's great Azhar mosque, and terrorize the people. The ringleaders were killed—"every night we have another thirty or so heads lopped off," as Bona-parte briskly put it—and order restored within two days. Napoleon estimated that seven hundred Egyptians had died; his chief of staff thought the figure more like four to five thousand.

The autumn months that followed brought only

silence from France and hostilities in Egypt. Ottoman armies were massing in Syria. To add to the general misery, bubonic plague began to spread among the troops. ("We lack nothing here," Bonaparte wrote home. "We are bursting with strength, good health, and high spirits.") By February he had decided to attack the Ottoman armies in Syria, using "the months of winter left to me in making the whole of the coast friendly through war and negotiation."

He marched an army of thirteen thousand northeast through the desert and captured Jaffa in a one-day siege on March 7, 1799. The city's fall was an orgy of murder; even worse was the fate of three thousand soldiers who surrendered with the promise that their lives would be spared. Bonaparte, who could not afford to feed them, ordered them all taken to the beach to be shot or bayoneted.

Haifa fell next, on March 16, but Bonaparte was then faced with Acre, just across the bay. An ancient crusader fortress commanded by an ancient rascal known as Djezzar ("the butcher") Pasha, Acre had a special advantage: the support of a small British squadron led by Captain Sir Sidney Smith and including a French émigré artillery expert. Acre held out for two bloody months, after which the French gave up. They withdrew to Cairo, lighting their way by torching villages and crops as they marched.

The army entered Cairo with bands playing and palms waving, preceded by a bulletin giving Bonaparte's version of events: "I razed Djezzar's Palace to the ground, along with the ramparts of Acre. There is not a stone left standing, and all the city's inhabitants have left

A posthumous portrait reveals the gruff and stout-hearted personality of Jean-Baptiste Kléber, commander of Bonaparte's army. Able, realistic, and outspoken, General Kléber began the expedition filled with admiration for Bonaparte's "vast genius"; in the end he felt only contempt for his commander in chief.

by sea." Even the troops had to laugh.

Within two weeks, as Bonaparte expected, Ottoman armies—backed again by the dashing Sir Sidney and his squadron—landed at Aboukir Bay. Bonaparte, having withdrawn troops from every part of Egypt for this battle, was waiting for them. His army was outnumbered by two to one, but Bonaparte's skill and General Joachim Murat's cavalry conferred an advantage. Murat's charges killed about two thousand of the adversary; four thousand more drowned in the bay, trying to reach their transports.

Bonaparte made the most of it in his bulletin: "The name of Aboukir was detested by every Frenchman before this battle took place; the events of July 25 have rendered it glorious," he wrote. "In a single operation we have made it possible for the French government to oblige England, in spite of her previous naval victories, to agree to a glorious peace with the Republic."

A panoramic view of the Battle of Aboukir (July 25, 1798) by Louis Lejeune shows the French rout of an attacking Turkish fleet. The Turks were driven by cavalry charges into Aboukir Bay, where four thousand drowned trying to reach their boats. Bonaparte wrote that the sea of bobbing turbans and dead men was "the most horrible thing I have ever seen."

*   *   *

During negotiations over prisoner exchange after the fight, Sir Sidney passed along the latest European newspapers, which revealed the wider repercussions of the Battle of the Nile. Paul I, the Russian czar, who fancied a role as grand master of the Knights Hospitalers, had been outraged by the capture of Malta. He sent his Black Sea fleet into the Mediterranean,

THE INSTITUTE OF EGYPT

"The true conquests, the only ones that leave no regrets, are those that have been wrested from ignorance," Bonaparte wrote before his departure for Egypt. He meant it. Before his expedition Egypt was unknown, except from the works of classical historians and of one or two modern travelers, which Bonaparte had absorbed with interest. His expedition explored this mysterious land as thoroughly as possible, and Bonaparte would always regard the expedition's intellectual achievements as the first among his accomplishments.

Those achievements were made possible by the remarkable group of civilian scholars Bonaparte took with him on the *Orient*. They were stars in their fields. Leading them was Bonaparte's friend, the mathematician Gaspard Monge; among other mathematicians was Jean-Baptiste Fourier, who created the system of mathematical analysis named for him. Other savants included the chemist Claude Berthollet, the zoologist Geoffroy Saint-Hilaire, the mineralogist Déodat de Dolomieu, and the artist Vivant Denon.

All of them worked at what came to be known as the Institute of Egypt, established by Bonaparte and housed in palaces outside Cairo. Here, despite the fact that much of their equipment disappeared with the *Orient*, they set up an observatory, botanical and zoological collections, an aviary, and a printing press.

Among their projects were practical ones such as improving the army's bread ovens, but most of their work was exploration of the geography, flora, fauna, and art of this almost unknown land. They surveyed and mapped Egypt. They explored, among other projects, the possibility of a Suez canal, of expanding irrigation, of damming the Nile, and of introducing new crops. They investigated Egypt's government, religion, and peoples, its insects, its ruins, its music, and most of all, its ancient monuments.

It was the institute that introduced the antiquities of the Nile to European eyes and fathered European archaeology. An army engineer found the Rosetta Stone, which with its triple inscriptions would provide clues to the content of ancient texts (right). It was the artist Vivant

Denon, following General Louis Desaix's division through Upper Egypt, who first recorded the wonders of Luxor, Karnak, and the Valley of the Kings. Arriving at sunrise at Thebes, even the exhausted army was impressed: they formed up, presented arms, and struck up the band.

Denon's drawings and his colleagues' discoveries would be presented to Europe in the *Description de L'Egypte*, published between 1809 and 1828 and rightly called monumental. It included ten huge volumes of plates, five devoted to antiquities, two to contemporary Egypt, and three to natural history; nine volumes of text; and three volumes of atlases and maps. With that vast work, the science of Egyptology was born.

Below: Vivant Denon made this drawing of the Pyramids at Giza. Members of the institute measure the Sphinx, whose features were much less eroded than they are today.

Right: The Rosetta Stone, found near the mouth of the Nile, displays a priest's decree inscribed in the hieroglyphics of Egyptian priests, the demotic characters of secular writers, and Greek. The triple inscription provided a key for Jean-François Champollion, who in 1832 made the first modern translation of ancient Egyptian texts.

where it took Corfu and the French Ionian islands. The British were besieging Malta. On the Continent, Austria had renewed war in March 1799; her armies were driving the French out of Germany and—with Russian help—out of Italy. France itself was in crisis, thanks to the political intrigues and corruption of the Directory.

Destiny clearly called. If France wanted to keep Egypt, she must be powerful in Europe, and Bonaparte was the man who could make her so. He therefore ordered his senior surviving admiral, Honoré Gan-

teaume, to prepare frigates for running the English blockade. On August 24, with a few aides and generals, Bonaparte deserted his army and sailed for France.

The expedition was planned in the deepest secrecy. Bonaparte left a letter behind ordering General Kléber to take command. Perhaps the general in chief did not care to face the blunt and by-now contemptuous Kléber, who had called him "that little bugger" and had observed that Bonaparte was the kind of general who needed an allowance of ten thousand men a month.

In this nineteenth-century painting by Louis Meyer, Bonaparte's return to France in 1799 becomes the romantic vision of a hero greeting his homeland. In reality, the general had deserted his troops in pursuit of his political destiny, but the romantic view prevailed and the hero of Aboukir was welcomed with shouts of acclaim.

Within a year Kléber fell to a Muslim assassin. Within another, the ragged remnants of the army of Egypt, now reduced by more than half, were defeated by British and Turkish forces and sent home at last to France.

*   *   *

In those two years and for thirteen more, Bonaparte's star of destiny was on the ascendant. He arrived in France on October 9, having sighted only one English sail. The news of his victory at Aboukir Bay had just preceded him: "No language can convey any idea of the state of excitement occasioned throughout France by Bonaparte's arrival . . . it amounted to a positive frenzy," a family friend recalled. "From the 9th of October all around us was in continual agitation." The Corsican arrived in Paris to the sweet sound of acclaim.

While the unpopular Directors might have liked to charge him with desertion, they did not dare. Instead, the various factions—radical, moderate, royalist—courted him, each seeking a sword to back a coup that would give it control of the government.

Bonaparte joined the moderate Emmanuel Sieyès. With Sieyès's party he overthrew the radical elements in the legislature on November 9 and 10. In the month that followed, Bonaparte effectively overthrew Sieyès, who had conceived a constitution providing for a strong executive—a consulate of three. Bonaparte allowed that constitution to stand, but altered it so that power resided in one consul, himself. Policy was developed by a council of state of forty-five to fifty men, and here Bonaparte showed genius. He chose experts for his council, insisting that the best men available, whatever their politics—and Napoleon's councils included men who had fought one another for ten years—work together. "I am national," he said. "I like honest men of all colors."

Bonaparte then transformed France, using the Council and his own unremitting work and sheer force of character—"the impetuous wind blowing about one's ears," one woman called it. The achievements in terms of strong, centralized government were staggering. They ranged from the badly needed reorganization of civil law in the famed Napoleonic Code to the creation of the Bank of France and the training of a competent civil service. The first consul also created awards for merit in the Legion of Honor; when an old revolutionary objected that decorations were "baubles," Bonaparte said with his usual cynicism that it was with baubles that people were governed: "The French are unable to desire anything seriously, except, perhaps, equality. Even so, they would gladly renounce it if everyone could entertain the hope of rising to the top. Equality in the sense that everyone will be master—there you have the secret of all your vanities."

As for foreign policy, it only added to his power. By warfare with the one and negotiation with the other, he created peace with both Austria and England in 1802. His reward was the first consulship for life, approved by plebiscite. Following a British-backed plot to assassinate him, he inspired a petition to create a hereditary

EGYPTOMANIA

The fashion for "Egyptian" design that swept Europe after Bonaparte's expedition was actually a revival of sorts. Europeans had drawn inspiration from the Nile at least since the fifth century B.C., when the Greek historian Herodotus wrote his famous account of the land that even then was seen as the fountainhead of ancient wisdom. In the next century Alexander the Great established the Ptolemies as Egypt's rulers. For almost three hundred years Alexandria, their peerlessly splendid capital with its famous library, remained the intellectual center of the Mediterranean, the conduit through which wisdom flowed west. The Romans, who conquered it in 30 B.C., were fascinated by Egyptian cults, Egyptian architecture, and Egyptian art: Rome imported them all and imitated them. The cult of the creative mother goddess, Isis, spread widely, for instance. Her temples were scattered throughout Rome's vast empire, along with Egyptian (or Egyptian-style) obelisks, pyramids (favored for tombs), and art objects.

Religious zealots created the catastrophe that broke the links with Egypt's venerable past. In 391, when the Christian Emperor Theodosius I ordered the closing of non-Christian temples throughout the empire, fanatics burned Alexandria's fabulous Temple of Serapis and—details are murky—a large portion of its seven hundred thousand volume library. Whatever survived of the vast collection of Pharaonic and Ptolemaic scholarship vanished in the Muslim fires of Arab conquest in 640.

After that, Egypt was essentially closed to the West. Even the understanding of hieroglyphic writing had been destroyed. Not that interest in the Egyptian style died. Remnants of earlier

France's famed Sèvres factory produced this porcelain inkwell in 1802. The designer managed to include a host of Egyptian motifs, including a typical column, invented hieroglyphs, sphinxes, and a lion.

glories, such as pyramids, obelisks, lions, and sphinxes, remained in Rome all during the Middle Ages; there was also a lively trade in mummies, which apothecaries ground to powder for use in medicines.

The Renaissance interest in antiquity—and exploration of Roman temples to Egyptian gods—sparked a small Egyptian revival that spread to France in the ornamental forms of palm-decorated columns, obelisks, and sphinxes. As a few French, British, and German travelers ventured once more into the unknown land, recording wonders like crocodiles and bananas, pyramids and temples, the fashion grew. By the eighteenth century, Egyptian style was seen as sublime—grand and terrifying, an architecture hinting at mysterious wisdom—especially in the hands of proselytizing artists like Giovanni Battista Piranesi and writers like Constantin-François Chasseboeuf, whose *Journey in Egypt and Syria* was in Bonaparte's traveling library.

It would take Bonaparte's expedition to produce accurate images of Egyptian art and architecture. These were first offered by Vivant Denon, leading artist among the general's savants, who in 1802 published the magnificent *Voyage in Lower and Upper Egypt During the Campaigns of General Bonaparte* in two huge volumes with superb engravings from his original drawings. The book was a bestseller. Translated into English and German, it went through forty editions.

In fact, it became the source book for Egyptian style all over Europe. The results were amazing: Egypt was

The Sèvres factory made this Egyptian tea service for Napoleon's empress, Josephine, in 1811. The empress had rejected a larger Egyptian dinner service as "too severe."

everywhere. There were Egyptian monuments with palm-topped columns and sphinxes; Bonaparte's victory monument in the Place du Chatelet in Paris is only one example. There were Egyptian "halls" like the one built in 1811 to house a museum of curiosities in London's Piccadilly; its statues and pylons sat oddly among its impeccable Georgian neighbors. Designers produced Egyptian rooms to house such furniture as boat-shaped couches with crocodile feet. Famous porcelain factories created Egyptian dinner services with gigantic centerpieces that featured temples flanked by obelisks. There were Egyptian-style libraries, gates, bridges, tombs, chimney pieces, and gardens with

stone sphinxes and pyramidal topiaries. The Antwerp Zoo even built an Egyptian temple to house its ostriches.

Not everyone approved of this Egyptian excess, but doubters seem to have been few. The English poet Robert Southey spoke for the minority when he wrote that after the Battle of the Nile, everything in England had to be Egyptian. He added that "the ladies wear crocodile ornaments and you sit upon a sphinx in a room hung round with mummies. . . . The very shopboards must be metamorphosed into the mode, and painted in Egyptian letters, which, as the Egyptians had no letters, you will doubtless conceive to be curious."

dynasty, again approved by plebiscite. He crowned himself emperor on December 2, 1804.

Well aware of the value of status and income, he
formed his own aristocracy as well. Leading it were his
own quarrelsome and avaricious siblings, for in true
Corsican fashion, Napoleon trusted only his family. In
the years of empire, he would put them on the thrones
of nations he conquered or created—Naples, Holland,
Westphalia, and Spain. He showered his mother with
honors too, but Letizia Bonaparte
remained stern, retiring, and
famously parsimonious. She
believed in the turns of destiny's
wheel: "I may one day have to find
bread for all these kings I have
borne" was the way she put it.

Then there was Josephine.
From a tumultuous beginning the
marriage had become one of
affection and support. Napoleon
saw her as the talisman of his destiny. She was his "superstition
rather than his love," Josephine
once said. "He considers me one of the rays of his star."
Even so, as his power and love of power grew, he tempt-
ed destiny. Josephine could not give him children. For
an heir and a great alliance, he divorced her in 1809 and
the next year married Marie Louise, daughter of the
emperor of Austria. She gave him an heir; the alliance
was short-lived.

It was his power that permitted the match between
the Corsican adventurer and the scion of the Hapsburgs.

Jacques-Louis David, who designed the costumes and decorations of the Cathedral of Notre Dame for Napoleon's self-coronation as emperor of the French, also painted this image of the dazzling ceremony. Incensed that he was not given special seats for the occasion, the once-fanatically Republican artist painted himself and his family into a gallery (center) above the emperor's mother, who did not attend.

From 1800 to 1814, Napoleon bestrode Europe like a colossus, defeating coalition after coalition in battles still commemorated in the names of streets, squares, and arches all over France: Marengo, Wagram, Austerlitz, Eylau.

Only rich England, ruler of the seas and paymaster of his enemies, steadily defied him, and his obsession with this adversary led him into blunders. He organized great armies for invasion, but he could not defeat the English at sea. In an attempt to weaken the island kingdom, he imposed the Continental System—a boycott of British trade—on Europe. Because Portugal refused to observe the system, he attacked—and ended up dangerously and expensively embroiled in Iberia. And in June

of 1812, partly because Russia withdrew from the system, he invaded with a grand army of four hundred and fifty thousand. By December forty thousand living skeletons, all that was left of the army after Russian battles and the Russian winter, straggled back toward France. Their emperor had left them behind to dash for Paris, fearing for his throne.

It was the beginning of the end. A sixth coalition of European powers formed in 1813; by 1814 it had invaded France in overwhelming numbers. The emperor was sent to exile on Elba, a pleasant island not far from Corsica. When he escaped in 1815, still charismatic enough to raise an army, all Europe declared him an outlaw and brought him down at the Battle of Waterloo.

His last gamble a failure, Napoleon sails to exile on St. Helena aboard the H.M.S. Northumberland. *This Orchardson print may refer to July 23, 1815, when Napoleon caught his last glimpse of Europe; he stayed at the rail from dawn to dusk, watching the coast fade away.*

This time the allies took no chances. Napoleon was sent to St. Helena, a cliff-girt 42 square miles of rock set in the South Atlantic, 1,200 miles from Africa. There he lived for six years with a small circle of supporters, closely guarded by the British. He spent his time rewriting his history, a revision that would make him a legend in France. In 1821 he died—of stomach cancer or a perforated ulcer or possibly of arsenic poisoning administered by a sycophant who hoped to inherit money from him.

In Napoleon's view, only England had prevented his becoming "the greatest man known to history." Even the ship that bore him into exile was English—the *Bellerophon,* as it happened, long since recovered from her battering by the *Orient* at Aboukir. His naval escorts found him charming. He told them, "In all my plans I have always been thwarted by the British fleet."

*   *   *

By the time Bonaparte uttered those words, the admiral who was the immortal emblem of English sea power had been dead a decade. Horatio Nelson did not live to see Napoleon's fall; even so, he was arguably more than any other man the author of it. The British fleet stood between the emperor and his destiny, and Nelson was the indomitable heart of the British fleet. War had mapped the trajectory of the two men's distant stars, and in the end, fortune favored not the soldier born to conquer but the sailor born to serve.

It was the Battle of the Nile that confirmed Nelson's ascendancy. A hero in England before the battle, Nelson was internationally renowned in the victory's wake. His government granted him a baronetcy; he was now Baron Horatio Nelson of the Nile and Burnham Thorpe. Bonfires burned across England in his honor, and Nelson memorabilia—mugs and engravings, model ships and Nelson dolls and illustrated books—sold out as fast as they could be produced. But if glory was abundantly his, it came at a price: the same glare that illuminated his virtues also delineated his flaws.

After the Nile it seemed to some that there were two Horatio Nelsons. The daring and brilliant commander, the inspirational leader, the warm and thoughtful friend, the plain-spoken parson's son and honorable apostle of king and country was still there; he would never be lost. But at his side there traveled an alter ego: a Nelson whose head was turned by flattery and meretricious show, whose passions made him capable of excess and cruelty, and whose vanity rendered this most esteemed of men almost, at times, ridiculous.

*   *   *

It was not until September 22 that the *Vanguard,* along with the *Culloden* and *Alexander,* limped into the Bay of Naples for repairs. By then the admiral was faring no better than his jury-rigged ship. The tension of the long search and the enduring effects of his battle wound had left him complaining of constant headaches and generally poor health. He thought of seeking leave to return to England to recover but dismissed the idea. Building on the victory at the Nile, England was reasserting her presence in the Mediterranean, and he was needed. Thus it was duty that first kept in him Naples, that lush and sensual city thought by ancient sailors to harbor sirens. But soon duty would not be the only draw, or even the major one.

He had not seen Emma Hamilton in five years, but she had written him from time to time, expressing her rapture after the Nile, for instance, in typically purple fashion: "Good God! What a victory! Never, never has there been anything half so glorious, half so complete!" She was now thirty-three, her once-perfect figure over-ripe and expanding daily. But she was still beautiful and still expert in deploying her assets. Of the luminaries who hailed Nelson's arrival in Naples, Emma sailed in the vanguard, rushing forward to swoon into his embrace with a cry of, "Oh, God, is it possible!"

The admiral became a guest at the Hamiltons' villa, and Emma set about staging entertainments for him that were lavish and tasteless enough to beggar even Naples' comic-opera style. Perhaps hung over from one of these, he wrote to St. Vincent that he hoped soon to be back at sea. "I am very unwell," he reported, "and the miserable conduct of this Court is not likely to cool my irritable temper. It is a country of fiddlers and poets,

Tricolored crocodiles fall beneath Horatio Nelson's club in a James Gillray caricature called Extirpation of the Plagues of Egypt. *The engraving reflects the popular acclaim in London for the hero of the Nile, but Nelson thought his official reward for the victory, a baronetcy, was rather deficient and that a viscountcy would have been more in order.*

whores and scoundrels." Apparently he had not yet succumbed to the humid blandishments of Naples, but he soon would. Before long he was dancing constant attendance on Emma, and tongues were beginning to wag.

Partly under her influence, Nelson also involved himself in Italian politics to an unwise and unwarranted degree, urging King Ferdinand to invade French-held Rome. The king took to the project with a certain lumpen enthusiasm, and his thirty thousand troops were able to oust the startled French—for about a week. Then they rallied and counterattacked, sending the Neapolitans scurrying home, with their king, disguised as a civilian, in the forefront of the flight. "The Neapolitan officers have not lost much honour, for God knows they had but little to lose," a disgusted Nelson observed, "but they lost all they had."

The incursion had served only to give the French a good excuse to attack Naples, which they did. In the dead of night, Nelson had to evacuate the huge royal family, its court, and the royal treasure in the *Vanguard*, making for Ferdinand's second capital, Palermo. The voyage was rough, crowded, and miserable. Amid lesser catastrophes, the last of Queen Maria Carolina's eighteen children, an infant, died during the crossing.

But Emma was in her element in all this turbulence and drama, and it was she who comforted the queen and rallied the other terrified passengers, displaying a spirit and courage that Nelson found awe-inspiring. If he had not been besotted with her before, he was now,

Among the rich gifts presented to Nelson by the Sultan of Turkey to commemorate the Nile victory were an elaborate musket and a shoulder-slung canteen. The silver cup memorializing the battle was a gift from the grateful Company of Merchants Trading in the Levant Seas.

and in Palermo their flirtation exploded into a full-fledged affair.

Nelson was venturing out of his depth in politics as well as love. Naples was briefly a battleground for royalist and republican forces, but Ferdinand's backers

167

A LADY WITH ATTITUDE

Ardent romantic that he was, it is hardly surprising that Horatio Nelson fell wildly in love with Emma Hamilton. Even by the standards of a romantic age, Emma was a stupendously romantic figure—gorgeous, passionate, scandalous.

The splendid infamy of her later years was hardly foreshadowed by her beginnings. She was a poor country girl, a blacksmith's daughter from a dreary hamlet in Cheshire. Her father died when she was an infant, and she was brought up in her grandmother's house in Wales. Emma was only twelve when she and her mother set out to better their circumstances in London. One of her first acts there was to change her name. She had been born Amy Lyon, but she began calling herself Emma Hart because she thought it sounded romantic.

It did, and it suited her. Her bumpkin accent (which she never lost) immediately telegraphed her deficiencies of birth and breeding, but if she was common, she was also adventurous—and breathtakingly lovely. Wide, violet eyes set off the perfect oval of her face, and she was tall and precociously voluptuous. Her luxuriant auburn hair fell nearly to her feet. In London she went briefly into domestic service and afterward, her critics would say, into common prostitution. But her looks destined her for something less dismal, and when she was just fifteen, she became the mistress of a young aristocrat about town, Sir Harry Fetherstonehaugh. There were stories of wild parties at his London house and of Emma dancing on tables, beguilingly naked. When she became pregnant, however, her protector threw her out, and she was taken in

Artist George Romney called this portrait of a pensive young Emma **Adriadne,** *after the heroine of a Greek myth.*

Sir William Hamilton willed this enamel miniature of his wife to Nelson. It was part of a locket that held a lock of Emma's auburn hair.

by another aristocrat, Charles Greville. Greville began cultivating his wild rose into something more suitable for a gentleman, and he cared for Emma's infant daughter until it was decided the child would be given to a foster family to rear.

Her new protector introduced Emma to the fringes, at least, of polite society, and her new friends included several artists who steered her toward her natural calling. She became an artist's model, and the finest English painters of the day vied for her services. Among them was George Romney, who called her "the Divine Emma" and fell in love with her. His many portraits of her—some demure, some frankly sensual—captured the youthful model at her most ravishing.

She loved the attention, but trouble

was brewing at home. Greville, the younger son of an earl but with no fortune of his own, needed to marry money. A mistress was an obstacle, so he sent Emma off to Naples to his widowed uncle, Sir William Hamilton, ambassador to the Neapolitan court. She was nineteen at the time; Hamilton was fifty-four. Emma, who truly loved Greville, thought her Neapolitan excursion was merely for acquiring more social graces. She soon grasped the truth of the situation, however, and she vowed that if she were to stay with Hamilton, it would be as his wife. Such a union was against all custom—gentlemen did not wed their mistresses—but the kindly Hamilton did marry her. He treasured her beauty, and he found good qualities in her character. If extravagant and flighty, she was nevertheless generous and good-hearted, and she tried to be a good wife. Always grateful to Hamilton for raising her to something approaching respectability, she did her best to make him proud. She learned Italian and French and became a great

favorite at court. There, among foreigners, her awful native accent went unnoticed, and it was only English visitors who covertly sneered.

The Hamiltons entertained often, and Emma favored her guests with singing in her strong (some said screeching) soprano. She also performed her famous "attitudes." These were tableaux vivant in which, using a few props, she gracefully portrayed classical and biblical figures. An attitude was apt to come upon her at almost any time. Once at a dinner party she fell off her chair in what appeared to be a dead faint, and her alarmed hostess was relieved when Hamilton explained that the swoon was merely an attitude in progress.

Emma seemed content with her role as Lady Hamilton, and apparently she was faithful to her elderly husband until Horatio Nelson came on the scene. Thereafter, the three settled into a *ménage* that was an open joke in England and a scandal to the upper classes, although it suited the participants: Hamilton had his wife's devotion, Nelson her passion, and each was happy. Hamilton politely

Merton Place, a seventy-acre country estate south of London, was bought by Nelson for himself and the Hamiltons in 1801 for £9,000. He had to borrow the purchase price, but "Paradise Merton," as he called it, was a beloved retreat. It was sold in 1808 to pay some of Emma's debts.

pretended that his wife and Nelson were merely friends, and when Emma had a child by her lover, he went along with the fiction that the little girl was their goddaughter. When Hamilton died both Nelson and Emma were by his bedside.

He left his widow with a comfortable income, and Nelson, in his will made before the Battle of Trafalgar, made her a "bequest to the Nation," trusting that king and country would see to her needs. His request was ignored by a disapproving establishment, however, and she chronically overspent her husband's legacy and was always in debt. Emma, Lady Hamilton, once hailed as the most beautiful woman in Europe, died at the age of fifty-three, a frowzy, penniless drunk.

eventually won out, and on June 24, 1799, the admiral and his squadron of seventeen ships sailed from Palermo to Naples to finish cleansing the city of French influence so the king and queen could return.

In his absence, Captain Edward Foote of the *Seahorse* had lent the British navy's imprimatur to a truce between the warring factions. Designed to save the city more mayhem at the hands of the departing French and their partisans, the agreement declared a general amnesty and safe conduct out of the kingdom for French sympathizers. But acting on royal orders to treat the dissidents like the rebels they were, Nelson annulled the terms of the truce. In so doing, he callously overrode a fellow officer's word of honor and also opened the door for a grisly series of executions. The hangings went on for days.

It was an ugly affair, and Nelson followed it up with brazen disobedience to a superior officer. Earl St. Vincent, aging and ailing, had by now left the Mediterranean for England, and his successor as commander in chief, George, Lord Keith, ordered

Nelson to send part of his squadron to help defend the island of Minorca. Nelson refused, declaring that Naples was more important than Minorca. Only after subsequent orders did he finally comply, sending three warships while he himself stayed behind, shuttling between Palermo and Naples, reveling in the attentions of Emma and the adulation of courtiers he had once scorned. His Neapolitan patrons had given him the dukedom of Bronte, a Sicilian estate in the foothills of Etna, and under the beaming royal gaze, the once-staid Nelson—resplendently decked out in his various medals and ribbons—drank too much champagne and stayed up too late, attending Emma at her evenings of extravagant gambling.

His precarious health was suffering, and so was his reputation, and his truest friends were relieved when, as the century turned, his romantic idyll was interrupted by news that the French were sending a small squadron to relieve their beleaguered garrison at Malta. The ships were said to include the *Généreux*, one of the escapees from the Nile. Nelson, his flag now in the 80-gun *Foudroyant*, set out in pursuit and captured her.

The venture gave a welcome glimpse of the old, heroic Nelson, but in London his superiors, concerned for his health and coldly disapproving of his liaison with Emma, ordered him home. "You will be more likely to recover your health and strength in England," wrote George, Lord Spencer, first lord of the Admiralty, "than in any inactive situation at a foreign Court, however pleasing the respect and gratitude shown to you for your services may be."

As it happened, the summons suited Nelson's own

Nelson loved fancy decorations and regalia, and his victory at the Nile added handsomely to his collection. The most famous was the chelengk, or plume of triumph, the highest Turkish award for valor. It was a spray of Brazilian diamonds with a large central stone that rotated on a clockwork mechanism. He wore it on his hat in place of a cockade, and it is prominent in the famous Lemuel Abbot portrait of the hero (left). Working from an earlier sketch, Abbot could only guess at the chelengk's appearance. He was also unaware that by now Nelson wore his hat tipped back on his forehead because of his head wound. Decorations on the admiral's coat are the Turkish Order of the Crescent (top, right), the Order of St. Ferdinand and Merit (center, left), and the Order of the Bath, which had been awarded him after the Battle of St. Vincent. Opposite is the hilt of an ornate sword given to him by the City of London to commemorate the Nile triumph.

plans. Sir William Hamilton was retiring to England in the summer of 1800, and the admiral planned to travel home with him—and, of course, with Emma. (Sir William had met his wife's infidelity with polite and worldly acceptance; he had known when he married a spectacular beauty thirty-six years his junior that the chance of her taking a lover sooner or later was hardly remote, and he seemed pleased that at least she had chosen a man he admired.)

This porcelain ice pail in the shape of a vase belonged to Nelson and bears his coat of arms. His name is on the shoulder of the piece above a swag containing the word Baltic, a reference to his victory at the Battle of Copenhagen in 1801.

Emma wanted to travel overland, so the odd cavalcade proceeded through Austria and Germany, making many stops. Everywhere Nelson was met with great applause, although in polite society Emma was either snubbed outright or coolly received by critics who afterward wrote scathingly to one another of her vulgarity, her size, her shameless parading of the overdressed Hero of the Nile like a trained monkey. After the entourage arrived in England on November 6, reactions were only magnified. Wildly enthusiastic crowds cheered Nelson's every appearance in public, but where esteem most mattered to him, there was little to be had. King George III received England's hero with ill-concealed contempt, and even the men closest to Nelson, many of his treasured fellow officers, were put off by his flagrant adultery. They were even more disgusted by the cold disdain that he displayed, even in public, toward his wife, a woman who had never wronged him in any way.

Nelson's boundless passion for his mistress survived all slights; he soon separated from Fanny and, after the Peace of Amiens, retired with the Hamiltons to a country house south of London. But he could not have been unmindful, or unmoved, by what that passion cost him. Earl St. Vincent, the inspirational mentor and patron who had helped mold Nelson into the hero he was, would in later years write of him: "Lord Nelson's sole merit was animal courage, his private character [was] most disgraceful in every sense of the word." Lest any miss his drift, St. Vincent added that Lady Hamilton was a "diabolical bitch."

* * *

Had matters ended in the aftermath of the Nile, Nelson might have been remembered, if at all, as an admiral who had scored one smashing victory before making himself a laughingstock over a woman. But, of course, matters did not end there.

In the spring of 1801, Nelson, now promoted to vice admiral, was dispatched as second in command on a vital mission to the Baltic. Russia's demented czar, Paul I, was now siding with France and had bullied Denmark, Norway, Sweden, and Prussia into the Armed Neutrality of the North, an alliance aimed at closing Baltic ports to the British. This was intolerable to England, whose navy relied on Baltic timber. In a daring and dangerous engagement with the Danish fleet at Copenhagen on April 2, Nelson won another dazzling triumph. Whatever his foibles ashore, at sea he was still brilliant.

In July 1801, the Admiralty named Nelson to command the anti-invasion forces in the English Channel, a post he held until October, when England and France ended hostilities with the Peace of Amiens. But the peace was brief. Britain declared renewed war on France in May of 1803, and Nelson was given command of the Mediterranean, his flag on the most renowned of the navy's first-rates, the 100-gun *Victory*.

By now Napoleon was massing troops at Boulogne, Brest, and Toulon to invade England. To succeed, however, he needed to control the English Channel long enough for a landing. His rather complicated plan to that end was to have his Atlantic and Mediterranean fleets sail for the West Indies, drawing off British ships in pursuit. In the New World the French fleets were to join forces and head back for Europe, there to unite with the allied Spanish fleet at Cádiz. With overwhelming numbers, the combined fleet would then seize the Channel. The invasion would proceed, and within a couple of days a French army would be marching on London.

Commanding the combined fleet would be Admiral Pierre Villeneuve, who had escaped from the Nile in the *Guillaume Tell*. Beginning in 1803, Nelson's fleet had kept Villeneuve bottled up at Toulon. But in March of 1805,

harried by Napoleon's demands for action, Villeneuve took advantage of bad weather to break out and head west. As he had once chased Brueys across the Mediterranean, Nelson now pursued Villeneuve across the Atlantic and back, but the French eluded any major battle and managed to enter Cádiz.

Villeneuve wanted a pitched battle with the English no more than Brueys had before him; he knew all too well the lethal implacability of British gunners. But the final showdown at sea, years in the making, was inevitable.

It came on the morning of October 21, 1805, off Cape Trafalgar on Spain's southern coast. The English captains were well drilled in their admiral's novel battle

Nelson wore this hat at the Battle of Copenhagen, the second of his three major victories. The defeat of the Danish fleet did not, however, bring him the same shower of honors that had followed the Nile. Denmark was technically a neutral country, and the British government was somewhat embarrassed by its hostile action against her.

plan: The British fleet would form into two lines and attack the rear and middle of the enemy line in perpendicular columns, one led by Nelson, the other by his old friend Cuthbert Collingwood. While the ships of the enemy van labored to turn back toward the battle, the British would annihilate the rearward men-of-war, then prepare to pick off the latecomers.

About 11:30 a.m., Nelson declared he would "amuse the fleet" with a message, and he instructed his signal lieutenant to hoist flags that read, "England Expects That Every Man Will Do His Duty." Many sailors and officers were baffled by the message. Of course they would do their duty; they always did. But they cheered heartily anyway, since it was their beloved Nelson sending the signal. It was followed by another one: "Close Action." Twenty-seven English ships of the line began moving forward. Thirty-three French and Spanish warships waited.

The first shots were fired at noon. Shortly thereafter, Nelson ordered his flag captain, Thomas Masterman Hardy, to run the *Victory* through the French line. She came so close to the *Redoutable* that the topmasts of the two ships locked, and they began pounding away at each other at point-blank range. It was the kind of toe-to-toe slugfest that the admiral had always liked best, and he saw about an hour of it from his quarterdeck before a marksman high in the *Redoutable*'s rigging shot him.

*Guns blazing, the **Victory** (center) smashes her way through the Franco-Spanish line, pouring a murderous hail of shot into the defenseless stern of the unfortunate French flagship **Bucentaure**. This painting by George Chambers captures the ferocity of the close-quarters battle that Nelson's daring tactics brought about.*

The musket ball entered his body at the shoulder and passed down through the pulmonary artery and lung before smashing through his spine to lodge in the muscles of his back below the right shoulder blade. Drowning in his own blood, forty-seven-year-old Horatio Nelson nevertheless held on for about three hours, long enough to be assured that he had won the greatest victory of his—or any admiral's—career. His last words, repeated over and over, were "Thank God I have done my duty."

No long-ago Viking ancestor raiding the Norfolk coast could have asked for a fairer passage to Valhalla.

In the cockpit of the Victory, the ship's chaplain rubs Nelson's chest to ease the pain of a mortal wound. Standing over his dying admiral in this A.W. Devis painting is Thomas Masterman Hardy, Nelson's flag captain and beloved friend.

*　　*　　*

Trafalgar did not stop Napoleon, who would continue for years to triumph on land. But Nelson's last battle—the last and greatest sea engagement of the Age of Sail—would assure British preeminence at sea for more than a century and would enable England to hold out against Bonaparte and, finally, to defeat him.

For Nelson, though, the war was over. He was carried home to a grieving England to be buried in a coffin that, oddly, had been with him for several years. One of his Band of Brothers, Captain Ben Hallowell, had had it fashioned for him as a sort of grisly joke, and it was one of the admiral's most cherished possessions. It was made of wood from the mainmast of the *Orient*.

THE IMMORTAL MEMORY

England learned of its hero's death on November 6, 1805, when a newspaper published a report from Nelson's friend, Admiral Cuthbert Collingwood, who had been second in command at Trafalgar. It told of the great triumph and of how dearly it had been bought—with the death of "a hero whose name will be immortal and his memory ever dear to his Country." From the royal palace to the lowest London slum, the grief was terrible. In Windsor Castle, King George III, who had so disapproved of Nelson's affair with Emma Hamilton, nevertheless wept for all the court to see. And in the pubs, merchants and chimneysweeps, barristers and blacksmiths, drank tearfully to the death of "Our Nel."

"The death of Nelson was felt in England as something more than a public calamity," the poet Robert Southey would write later; "men started at the intelligence and turned pale; as if they had heard of the loss of a dear friend. An object of our admiration and affection, of our pride and of our hopes . . . it seemed as if we had never, till then, known how deeply we loved and reverenced him." Nowhere was the mourning more poignant than in the British fleet. "I never set eyes on him," a sailor in the *Royal Sovereign* wrote home, "for which I am both sorry and glad; for to

be sure I should like to have seen him, but then, all the men in our ship who have seen him are such soft toads, they have done nothing but Blast their Eyes and cry ever since he was killed. God bless you! Chaps that fought like the Devil, sit down and cry like a wench!"

It was his flagship that brought Nelson home. The body had been put into one of the ship's water casks, which was filled with brandy mixed with camphor and myrrh and lashed to the *Victory*'s mainmast. She arrived at Portsmouth on December 5 and proceeded on to the Downs off Deal, where the body was dressed in uniform and placed into the coffin made from the *Orient*'s mainmast. This was sealed in lead and placed inside a second wooden casket. On Christmas Eve a yacht ferried the body to Greenwich Hospital, where, in a richly decorated black outer coffin, it lay in state for three days in early January 1806, while more than thirty thousand mourners filed by.

Thousands more lined the banks of the Thames on January 8 as the hero, borne on a black-canopied funeral barge escorted by a 2-mile-long procession of barges, moved upriver against a strong southwest wind on the 6-mile trip to the Admiralty at Whitehall. As the coffin was landed at Whitehall Stairs, a hailstorm broke. The next day dawned clear and cold, however, as London prepared to bid Nelson goodbye with a funeral whose pomp and magnitude had theretofore been reserved only for kings.

Under lowering skies, Lord Nelson's funeral procession moves along the Thames from Greenwich to Whitehall in a painting by J. M. W. Turner. Despite the cold, threatening weather, thousands of mourners turned out to see the somber flotilla and pay their last respects.

The funeral procession was so long that the beginning of it reached St. Paul's Cathedral before the carriages that brought up its rear had left the Admiralty more than a mile and a half away. At its head was a troop of Light Dragoons, their horses' slow hoofbeats muffled by sand that workmen had spread along the streets. Behind them came four regiments of infantry, some ten thousand men, most dressed in black shakos and red jackets. They marched to the mournful strains of the "Dead March" from Handel's *Saul*, played on pipes and trumpets. Following were forty-eight crewmen from the *Victory* carrying ragged Union Jacks and Nelson's St. George ensign. England's peers and nobles marched behind, as did the Prince of Wales, all of them proud to honor a poor parson's son from Norfolk.

At last came Nelson's magnificent funeral car, drawn by six horses in plumed headdresses. Memorializing Trafalgar, it was shaped like the *Victory*, with a winged prow ornament representing Fame; but it also bore reminders of the Battle of the Nile. The capitals of the columns supporting its enormous sable canopy were in the form of palm fronds. As it made its stately way through the streets, silence pervaded the huge crowd that watched. There were only

A prayerbook was specially produced for Nelson's four-hour funeral service at St. Paul's Cathedral. A ticket to the service was placed inside the front cover.

the sounds of weeping and the occasional whisper of "God bless" or "Hats off."

The winter sun was fading as the four-hour funeral service began inside St. Paul's, and the packed cathedral's cavernous dome had to be lit artificially for the first time in its history. In the glow of a chandelier blazing with candles, choirs sang "I Am the Resurrection and the Life" and other hymns, and eulogies were delivered. The climax of the ceremony came when Nelson's crew from the *Victory* stepped forward and laid his

An engraving of Lord Nelson's funeral car shows details memorializing his two most famous battles. The prow ornament and stern of the Victory *represent Trafalgar, and the palm trees atop the columns and palm fronds crossed on the side recall the Nile.*

shot-rent ensign atop his casket to be interred with him—but not before each of them tore off a bit of it and put it into his jacket, next to his heart. The body of Vice Admiral Horatio, Lord Nelson was finally laid to rest beneath the great dome, encased in a princely sarcophagus that had originally been purchased by Cardinal Wolsey, chancellor of England in the time of King Henry VIII. In front of it, inlaid in the cathedral's marble floor, is the inscription: "England Expects That Every Man Will Do His Duty."

The grief at Nelson's death and the love that inspired the grief were slow to fade in England, where his faults were swallowed up in memory of his virtues and the grandeur of his death. Popular poems and plays and ballads,

commemorative snuffboxes and plates and samplers and tea canisters faded soon enough, but more enduring monuments remained. Trafalgar Square was laid out to honor him, at its center a 145-foot-high column bearing a 17-foot-tall statue of him. Ships, and even towns, were christened after him, and in London alone there are still nearly fifty roads, streets, places, walks, rows, squares, passages, or terraces that bear his name.

Over the Royal Navy, especially, his spirit still hovers, a unique avatar of all that men who serve at sea might ever aspire to become. So it is that to this day, on the anniversary of Trafalgar, men of the fleet, wherever they may be, raise a glass and join in a toast: "To the immortal memory."

The Fleet Recovered

*I*N THE YEARS SINCE the Battle of the Nile, countless divers sought, without success, the drowned relics and treasures hidden in the depths of Aboukir Bay. Only in 1983, when marine explorer Jacques Dumas began surveying the region with the help of the French navy, would the wreckage of Napoleon's flagship, the 124-gun *Orient*, and that of the *Artémise*, a 40-gun frigate, be found.

Dumas later invited Franck Goddio, who was then conducting a study of worldwide underwater archaeological efforts, to dive with him at the site. Dumas recovered a number of artifacts, shown on the following pages, but he did not live to see the full extent of the treasures yielded by the wreckage. He died just a few months after Goddio's first dive with him.

The site remained undisturbed for more than a decade, until 1996, when Goddio, by then head of the European Institute for Underwater Archaeology, began a satellite survey of the bay. He again located both the *Orient* and the *Artémise* and discovered a third shipwreck, the *Sérieuse*. Two years later, at the request of the Egyptian Supreme Council for Antiquities, Goddio relaunched the Battle of the Nile excavation initiated by Dumas, uncovering a trove of nautical and personal objects that provide a window into life at sea and at war at the close of the eighteenth century.

Left: Planking and couplings long since disintegrated and nail holes gaping, the once-proud bow of the Orient *lies stripped down to its copper sheeting.*
Above: A small bell, probably used by the ship's chaplain to conduct Catholic mass aboard the Orient. *Seagoing clergymen were scarce; those who would sail were afforded senior warrant officer status and assigned to the best ships.*
Previous page: Like an underwater apparition, a cannon found at the site of the Orient *is investigated by a diver.*

185

Above: The support vessel Princess Duda *hovers over the* Orient *wreckage site. Goddio's team brought their discoveries to the surface for logging and study by archaeological experts. They were then transported to Egypt for restoration at the Laboratory of the Supreme Council for Antiquities in Alexandria.*

Above: Preparation is everything for (left to right) divers Jean-Paul Blancan, Patrice Sandrin, and Daniel Visnikar, here studying the excavation map of the Orient.

Right: Goddio confers with team member Susan Hendrickson over a well-preserved spyglass from the Orient. *The* Orient's *lookout, perched in the crosstrees, might have caught sight of Nelson's brazen brigade using a similar glass.*

At first, Goddio despaired during his first dive with Dumas when he saw the inscription on this bronze rudder holder: "Dauphin Royal" *(above and left)*. *But a quick history lesson from Dumas confirmed that this was, indeed,* Napoleon's Orient—*the* Royal Dolphin, *a term used by the French to refer to the heir to the throne, had been the* Orient's *name before the Revolution.*

Right: Twin rings from the Orient's *main mast ironically reflect the circle's symbolism of eternity: Admiral Nelson was later buried in a casket made from the* Orient's *wooden mast. With much amusement, he had accepted the coffin as a gift from the captain of the* Swiftsure, *one of the ships under his command, and kept it the rest of his life. Nelson now lies in that same coffin in Saint Paul's Cathedral, London.*

Upper left: A chunk of gilded wood attests to the gold ornamentation that graced the bow of the Orient.

Left: Down in the bowels of the ship, one of four bilge pump holes near the main mast remarkably still bears some of the rope wrapping used to make the pump waterproof.

Above: Artist Patrice Sandrin uses waterproof drawing tools to sketch the site for later review by scholars. The locational grid lines help the team identify the exact location of artifacts.

189

Before shooting a large cannon or a smaller carronade (left) the ship's crew would set off a miniature version (below) to test the readiness of the gunpowder. This tester was retrieved from the wreckage of the French Sérieuse. Napoleon's fleet actually packed much more firepower than Nelson's—but the element of surprise and the tactical brilliance of the British commander proved to be the greater weapons in the end. A 36-pound cannon, the largest marine cannon, required fifteen men to operate. Preparations for each shot took eight minutes.

Left: *These air-filled lift bags won't raise this iron cannon, a 36-pounder found on the* Orient, *straight to the surface. Rather, the buoys help move heavy artifacts off the floor and into position for lifting by cranes stationed on the* Princess Duda, *avoiding a drag-and-scrape along the bottom that*

might damage the relics. The massive iron cannons that studded every fighting ship were termed according to the weight of the cannonballs they could handle, not the true weight of the cannon itself. (A 9½-foot-long 36-pounder, the largest marine cannon, actually weighed nearly 4 tons.)

Above: Chief diver Jean-Claude Roubaud steadies a bronze carronade as it is lifted on board the support vessel for examination. A carronade, the smallest gun on a ship, was located on the upper deck.

Inset left: The etching "Jean Batiste Martinenq" denotes the name of the proud caster of the gun. Inset right: The engraved French port and date, "Toulon, May 1788," pinpoints the location and date of its manufacture.

When the Orient's magazines met flame (sparked by enemy fire but fanned by paint and other flammable liquids left lying about the deck), the blast temporarily silenced the battle and sent nearly all the ship's crew and contents to the ocean floor. So fierce was the explosion— the heat alone melted the tar between the planks of the ship next to it—that an officer's sword was sent tearing to the bottom of the bay, where it slammed into the sand (left).

Both the embedded sword (above) and a lone sword shield (right) were retrieved by the divers.

A passing jellyfish, looking peculiarly like an air-filled lift bag (below) floats above a 36-pounder cannon. Piles of 36- and 24-pound iron shot (inset) were scattered throughout the site. The proximity in which warring ships fought meant that a single cannonball might easily blast through one side of the opponent's hull and out the other. A cannonball shot from about 200 feet could blast through 35 inches of solid oak.

Diver Alaa El Din Mahrous finds an intact musket (above) that saw action on the Sérieuse. Meanwhile, Nicolas Ponzone (right) sifts through thick sediment near where the Orient came to rest, and harvests scores of spent lead shot. Lurking there as well may be remnants of langrage, shrapnel-like ammunition that could be stuffed into the cannons. Langrage shot consisted of metal shards—nails, chains, and various bits of iron—jumbled together into a vicious cylinder designed to shred enemy sails. One such projectile gashed Admiral Nelson's head midway through the battle, leading him to think he was mortally wounded.

Just over 100 yards from the remains of the Orient are the shaft and ring (inset, left) of the Tonnant's main anchor, (left) one of seven found in the immediate area. As the Orient threatened to turn into a fireball, the captains of the other French ships ordered their anchors to be cut so they could flee. This helped some ships escape altogether, while causing others to run aground in the shallow bay.

Thirty-six feet long, the rudder of the Orient still bears its protective copper sheeting (above). But its wooden components have been eaten away; only bronze reinforcement plates and nails (left) remain, draped by the security chain once attached to the Orient's stern.

The Orient *sailed with a well-stocked pharmacy. Powders and potions may have been stored in sturdy bottles (right) such as the intact one found here, and then poured into containers such as these delicately engraved crystal vials (left and below) which somehow escaped being shattered. The large ladle (above) may have come from the pharmacy or the kitchen.*

Life at sea may have been difficult, but men of certain rank enjoyed a bit of refinement in their daily routine. Among the finds (clockwise from left): a French ceramic dish, glazed and decorated with a bird on a tree branch; a fork and spoon from the Orient's officers' table, bearing hallmarks of eighteenth-century French silversmiths (inset); a crystal salt cellar (the salt would have been spooned out).

Personal effects poignantly speak of the men behind the uniforms. Diver Eric Smith gingerly examines the remnants of a leather shoe (above). In this medley of brass and bone buttons (above right) are some that indicate the regiment number of the soldier or officer wearing them. This gold filigree ornament (right) and a gold belt buckle (opposite, middle) were also found at the site, the latter in the ship's stern. A number of the men who survived the Orient's explosion (fewer than eighty, by one account) were found naked when they were rescued by the British, their clothing either blown or burned off.

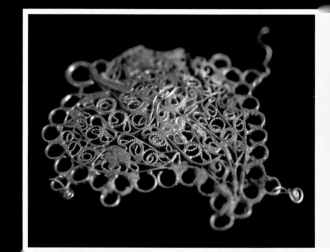

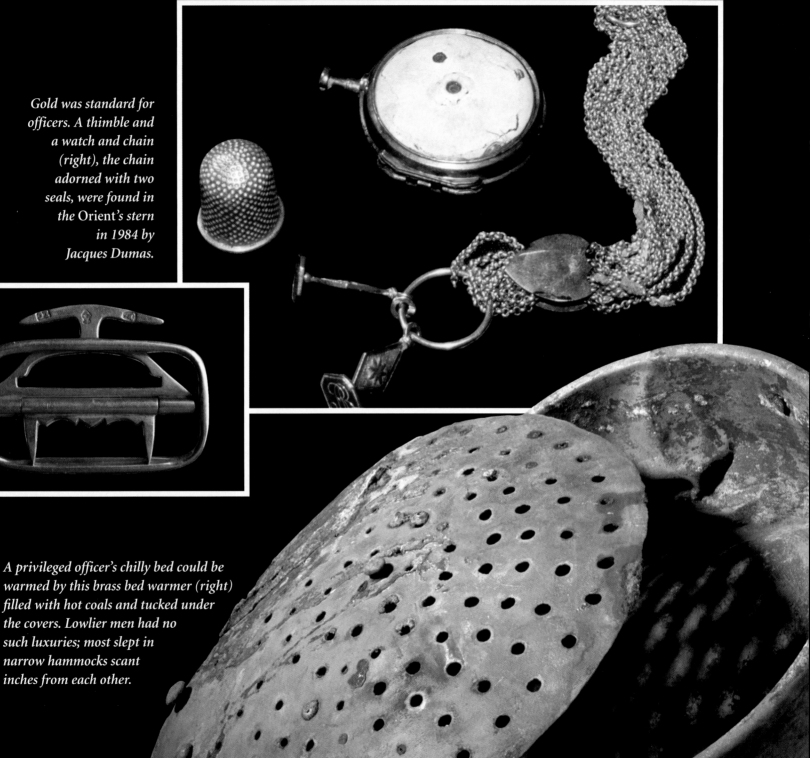

Gold was standard for officers. A thimble and a watch and chain (right), the chain adorned with two seals, were found in the Orient's stern in 1984 by Jacques Dumas.

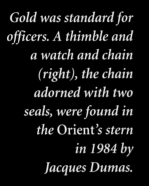

A privileged officer's chilly bed could be warmed by this brass bed warmer (right) filled with hot coals and tucked under the covers. Lowlier men had no such luxuries; most slept in narrow hammocks scant inches from each other.

Underwater archaeologists rarely find actual human remains—typically, not even bone can withstand the salt water, marine life, and other destructive elements. This intact jawbone, complete with cavity-ridden teeth, was found under the Orient— suggesting to archaeologist Alaa El Din Mahrous (above) that the man's body had been pinned beneath the ship when it settled on the ocean floor.

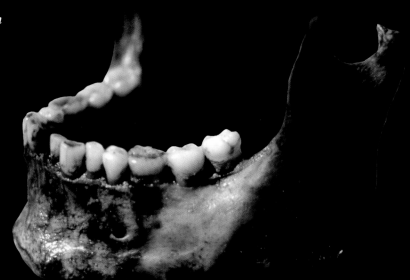

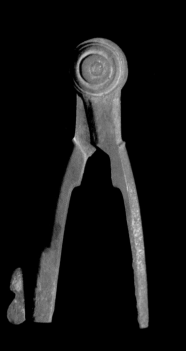

Alain Peton (above) holds a spyglass found on the Orient. *Such simple optical equipment was employed to sight land and other ships.*

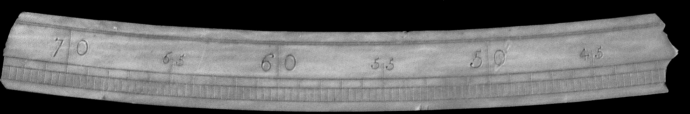

Relics that hint of the workaday business aboard the Orient *and* Sérieuse *include these compasses (above, left) and a portion of an ivory octant (above) used for plotting the ship's course.*

Bonaparte ordered that a printing press be carried on board the Orient *to publish his declarations once he installed himself in Egypt. Divers located a few remaining letters and other bits of lead type.*

Philippe Rousseau (above) uncovers gold coins during the excavation of the *Orient's* stern. The number of pre-Revolutionary coins found on the *Orient*, including ones bearing the likeness of French King Louis XV (far right) and Louis XVI (immediate right) attest to the toll the Revolution was taking on France's economy: the gold in these coins was valuable, offering a counter to the wild inflation that occurred after the Revolution.

A diver holds four gold coins from eighteenth-century Istanbul and a button.

Recovered from the Orient are some unusual surprises for a French ship: gold coins from Malta, Portugal, Spain, Venice, Istanbul, and other sovereignties. The variety of these foreign coins led Goddio to believe that they are all that remain of the trove pilfered during the French conquest of Malta en route to Egypt. Most of the treasure was probably carried ashore by the French when they reached Alexandria. Much of it was sent back to France on the Sensible, which later was also captured by the British.

Inset above: Venetian ducats.
Right: Single coins and two piles of ornate coins from the Ottoman Empire.

Front and back sides of coins,
top to bottom: a Portuguese
coin depicting Johannes V,
dated 1733; a Maltese coin
picturing Emmanuel de
Rohan, great master of the
order of Malta; another
Portuguese coin, this one of
King Joseph I, dated 1772.

BIBLIOGRAPHY

Abrantes, Laure Junot, duchesse d'. *At the Court of Napoleon: Memoirs of the Duchesse d'Abrantes.* New York: Doubleday, 1989.

Battesti, Michele. *La Bataille d'Aboukir 1798.* Paris: Economica, 1998.

Bourrienne, Louis Antoine Fauvelet. *Memoires de M de Bourrienne sur Napoleon.* Paris: Garnier, 1899-1900.

Bradford, Ernle. Nelson: *The Essential Hero.* New York: Harcourt Brace Jovanovich, 1977.

Bruce, Evangeline. *Napoleon and Josephine: An Improbable Marriage.* New York: Scribner, 1995.

Carrington, Dorothy. *The Dream Hunters of Corsica.* London: Weidenfeld & Nicholson, 1995.

Curl, James Stevens. *Egyptomania: The Egyptian Revival: A Recurring Theme in the History of Taste.* Manchester and New York: Manchester University Press, 1994.

Deane, Anthony. *Nelson's Favourite: HMS Agamemnon at War 1781-1809.* Annapolis, Md.: Naval Institute Press, 1996.

The Editors of Horizon Magazine. *The Horizon Book of the Age of Napoleon.* New York: American Heritage Publishing, 1963.

The Editors of Time-Life Books. *The Divine Campaigns: 1100-1200.* Amsterdam: Time-Life Books, 1989.

Gardiner, Robert, ed. *Nelson Against Napoleon: From the Nile to Copenhagen, 1798-1801.* Annapolis, Md.: Naval Institute Press, 1997.

Hibbert, Christopher. *Nelson: A Personal History.* Reading, Mass.: Perseus Books, 1994.

Lavery, Brian. *Nelson and the Nile: The Naval War Against Bonaparte 1798.* Annapolis, Md.: Naval Institute Press, 1998.

Markham, Felix. *Napoleon.* New York: Penguin Books, 1963.

Moreh, Shmuel, trans. *Al-Jabarti's Chronicle of the French Occupation, 1798.* Princeton and New York: Markus Wiener Publishing, 1993.

O'Brian, Patrick. *Men-of-War.* New York: W.W. Norton & Company, 1974.

Pocock, Tom. *Nelson and His World.* New York: Viking Press, 1968.

Pope, Dudley. *Life in Nelson's Navy.* Annapolis, Md.: Naval Institute Press, 1987.

Pope, Steve. *Hornblower's Navy: Life at Sea in the Age of Nelson.* New York: Welcome Rain, 1998.

Schama, Simon. *Citizens: A Chronicle of the French Revolution.* New York: Vintage Books, 1989.

Schom, Alan. *Napoleon Bonaparte.* New York: HarperPerennial, 1997.

Tracy, Nicholas. *Nelson's Battles: The Art of Victory in the Age of Sail.* Annapolis, Md.: Naval Institute Press, 1995.

Whipple, A.B.C. *Fighting Sail.* Alexandria, Va.: Time-Life Books, 1978.

White, Colin. *1797: Nelson's Year of Destiny.* Phoenix Mill, Thrupp, Stroud, Gloucestershire: Sutton Publishing Ltd., 1998.

——, ed. *The Nelson Companion.* Annapolis, Md.: Naval Institute Press, 1995.

INDEX (**Boldface** *indicates pages with illustrations.*)

PICTURE CREDITS